Microwave Magic
Desserts

Grolier Limited
TORONTO

Contributors to this series:

Recipes and Technical Assistance:
École de cuisine Bachand-Bissonnette
Cooking consultants:
Michèle Emond, Denis Bissonnette
Photos:
Laramée Morel Communications
Audio-Visuelles
Design:
Claudette Taillefer
Assistants: Joan Pothier
Julie Deslauriers
Philippe O'Connor
Accessories: Andrée Cournoyer
Editing: Communications
La Griffe Inc.

Assembly: Marc Vallières
Vital Lapalme
Carole Garon
Jean-Pierre Larose
Production Manager:
Gilles Chamberland
Art Director:
Bernard Lamy
Consultants:
Roger Aubin
Joseph R. De Varennes
Gaston Lavoie
Jocelyn Smyth
Donna Thomson
Production:
Le Groupe Polygone Éditeurs Inc.

The series editors have taken every care to ensure that the information given is accurate. However, no cookbook can guarantee the user successful results. The editors cannot accept any responsibility for the results obtained by following the recipes and recommendations given.

Canadian Cataloguing in Publication Data

Desserts
(Microwave magic ; 3)
Translation of: Les Desserts.
Includes index.
ISBN 0-7172-2377-9

1. Microwave cookery.   2. Desserts.
I. Series: Microwave magic (Toronto, Ont.) ; 3.

TX832.D3813 1987   641.5'882   C87-094419-3

Table of Contents

Each of the twenty-six volumes is devoted to a particular type of cooking for ease of reference. So, if you are looking for dessert recipes, you simply go to one of the volumes on that subject. Each volume has its own index, and the final volume will contain a general index to the complete series.

The series puts over one thousand two hundred recipes at your fingertips. You will find it as useful as the microwave oven itself. Enjoy!

Note from the Editor

How to Use this Book
The books in this set have been designed to make your job as easy as possible. As a result, most of the recipes are set out in a standard way.

We suggest that you begin by consulting the information chart for the recipe you have chosen. You will find there all the information you need to decide if you are able to make it: preparation time, cost per serving, level of difficulty, number of calories per serving and other relevant details. Thus, if you have only 30 minutes in which to prepare the evening meal, you will quickly be able to tell which recipe is possible and suits your schedule.

The list of ingredients is always clearly separated from the main text. When space allows, the ingredients are shown together in a photograph so that you can make sure you have them all without rereading the list—

another way of saving your valuable time. In addition, for the more complex recipes we have supplied photographs of the key stages involved either in preparation or serving.

All the dishes in this book have been cooked in a 700 watt microwave oven. If your oven has a different wattage, consult the conversion chart that appears on the following page for cooking times in different types of oven. We would like to emphasize that the cooking times given in the book are a minimum. If a dish does not seem to be cooked enough, you may return it to the oven for a few more minutes. Also, the cooking time can vary according to your ingredients: their water and fat content, thickness, shape and even where they come from. We have therefore left a blank space on each recipe page in which you can note

the cooking time that suits you best. This will enable you to add a personal touch to the recipes that we suggest and to reproduce your best results every time.

Although we have put all the technical information together at the front of this book, we have inserted a number of boxed entries called **MICROTIPS** throughout to explain particular techniques. They are brief and simple, and will help you obtain successful results in your cooking.

With the very first recipe you try, you will discover just how simple microwave cooking can be and how often it depends on techniques you already use for cooking with a conventional oven. If cooking is a pleasure for you, as it is for us, it will be all the more so with a microwave oven. Now let's get on with the food.

The Editor

Key to the Symbols
For ease of reference, the following symbols have been used on the recipe information charts.

The pencil symbol ✏️ is a reminder to write your cooking time in the space provided.

Level of Difficulty

🍴 Easy

🍴🍴 Moderate

🍴🍴🍴 Complex

Cost per Serving

$ Inexpensive

$ $ Moderate

$ $ $ Expensive

Power Levels

All the recipes in this book have been tested in a 700 watt oven. As there are many microwave ovens on the market with different power levels, and as the names of these levels vary from one manufacturer to another, we have decided to give power levels as a percentage. To adapt the power levels given here, consult the chart opposite and the instruction manual for your oven.

Generally speaking, if you have a 500 watt or 600 watt oven you should increase cooking times by about 30% over those given, depending on the actual length of time required. The shorter the original cooking time, the greater the percentage by which it must be lengthened. The 30% figure is only an average. Consult the chart for detailed information on this topic.

Power Levels

HIGH: 100% - 90%	Vegetables (except boiled potatoes and carrots) Soup Sauce Fruits Browning ground beef Browning dish Popcorn
MEDIUM HIGH: 80% - 70%	Rapid defrosting of precooked dishes Muffins Some cakes Hot dogs
MEDIUM: 60% - 50%	Cooking tender meat Cakes Fish Seafood Eggs Reheating Boiled potatoes and carrots
MEDIUM LOW: 40%	Cooking less tender meat Simmering Melting chocolate
DEFROST: 30% **LOW: 30% - 20%**	Defrosting Simmering Cooking less tender meat
WARM: 10%	Keeping food warm Allowing yeast dough to rise

Cooking Time Conversion Chart

700 watts	600 watts*
5 s	11 s
15 s	20 s
30 s	40 s
45 s	1 min
1 min	1 min 20 s
2 min	2 min 40 s
3 min	4 min
4 min	5 min 20 s
5 min	6 min 40 s
6 min	8 min
7 min	9 min 20 s
8 min	10 min 40 s
9 min	12 min
10 min	13 min 30 s
20 min	26 min 40 s
30 min	40 min
40 min	53 min 40 s
50 min	66 min 40 s
1 h	1 h 20 min

* There is very little difference in cooking times between 500 watt ovens and 600 watt ovens.

Sweet Treats

Sweet treats . . . this term can be applied to a whole range of delightful cakes, pastries, breads, muffins and other desserts. We have exotic creations for special occasions, comfort foods for dull days and tasty treats for every day. For most of us, a meal without dessert is not complete. Desserts are a central part of our culinary culture, but they have been popular throughout history as well.

People have been using flour as a basic ingredient in dessert preparation for centuries. Research has shown that even in ancient times the Egyptians made cakes from a simple yeast dough sweetened with fruit, sugar and honey. From such modest beginnings cooks quickly developed an impressive repertoire of breads, cakes and cookies.

Between the seventeenth and nineteenth centuries, cooking developed into an art in its own right and desserts came to be highly esteemed. It was during this period that people developed more sophisticated

tastes and sought greater variety in their food. The heavy and highly spiced dishes of days gone by were gradually replaced with lighter dishes prepared in a variety of ways. Desserts were part of this general trend.

The preparation of cakes, pastries and other desserts has become a specialty in many culinary traditions. However, you don't have to be a master pastry chef to produce excellent results yourself. And while it is certainly quicker to buy a ready-made loaf or cake, nothing can beat the satisfaction of biting into something you have created yourself. Besides, you can then be sure that it was made with fresh ingredients— bought products, frequently made with dehydrated ingredients and artificial flavorings, just cannot match the taste of those that are made at home.

There is no end to the number of simple recipes that can be adapted to suit the particular preferences of the

people you cook for. In this volume you will find a variety of recipes to suit every taste. You can easily improvise on them, making your own personal adaptations and creating desserts that are bound to bring you extra compliments. You will also discover the extent to which using a microwave oven will simplify their preparation. In less time than it takes to heat a conventional oven, you will be able to make a dozen cookies in the microwave! Thus you need never be caught with nothing to offer surprise guests. And don't forget that many of the conventional recipes you have been using can easily be adapted to this revolutionary method of cooking, which is extraordinarily easy in spite of what many people think.

Just relax and give your imagination free rein!

Adapting Recipes

Must you throw out all your conventional recipes when you install a microwave oven? Of course not! Most conventional recipes can easily be adapted for use in the microwave. To do this, however, you must keep in mind a few basic principles on microwave cooking and how it differs from conventional cooking. The action of the microwaves on different foods are described at various points throughout this volume.

On your first attempt to adapt a recipe to the microwave oven, be sure to choose one that you know well. It will be much easier to work out the changes that are required if you know what the final result should be. If you want to adapt a recipe with which you are not familiar, try to assess whether or not it is likely to give the result you want. If a particular dish is not to your liking when prepared in the conventional way, it is not likely to appeal to you any more when cooked in the microwave oven.

Consider the following example of apple pie. Boldface type is used to show the differences between the conventional recipe and that adapted for use in the microwave.

Apple Pie—
Conventional Recipe

Pastry:
500 mL (2 cups)
all-purpose flour

5 mL (1 teaspoon)
salt

150 mL (2/3 cup)
vegetable shortening

45 to 60 mL (3 to 4 tablespoons)
butter or margarine

90 mL (6 tablespoons)
cold water

Filling:
175 mL (3/4 cup)
sugar

50 mL (1/4 cup)
flour

2 mL (1/2 teaspoon)
ground nutmeg

2 mL (1/2 teaspoon)
ground cinnamon

pinch
salt

1.5 L (6 cups)
apple, peeled and sliced

— Combine the flour and salt. Use a pastry blender to cut the shortening and butter into the flour and salt. Use a pastry blender to cut the shortening and butter into the flour until the mixture resembles coarse crumbs. Add the water gradually, stirring constantly with a fork until the dough forms a stiff lump. **Divide the dough into two equal portions and shape each into a ball. Set one ball aside.**
— Flatten the other ball until it is 1.25 cm (1/2 inch) thick and then, with a rolling pin, roll the pastry out to form a circle 4 mm (1/8 inch) thick.
— Place on a 22.5 cm (9 inch) pie plate, making sure that the pastry extends 2.5 cm (1 inch) over the edge all around.
— Trim the edge to 1.25 cm (1/2 inch). **Set the pie crust aside.**
— Put all the filling ingredients except the apple slices into a bowl and mix. Add the apple and mix again, thoroughly. Spoon the filling into the pie crust.
— **Roll out the other ball of pastry to form a circle 4 mm (1/8 inch) thick. Place over the filling, dampen with a little cold water and press together. Crimp the edges and make a few cuts in the top.**
— **Bake for 40 to 50 minutes, or until the juices in the filling boil.**

Basic Principles for Adapting Recipes

Ingredients:
Liquid ingredients slow microwave cooking down whereas fatty ingredients speed it up. To adapt a conventional recipe you must reduce the amount of liquid and fat to obtain the right balance between the two.

Apple Pie—
Recipe Adapted for Microwave Cooking

Pastry:
250 mL (1 cup)
all-purpose flour

2 mL (1/2 teaspoon)
salt

75 mL (1/3 cup)
vegetable shortening

15 to 30 mL (1 to 2 tablespoons)
butter or margarine

30 to 45 mL (2 to 3 tablespoons)
cold water

3 to 4 drops
yellow food coloring

Filling:
175 mL (3/4 cup)
sugar

50 mL (1/4 cup)
flour

2 mL (1/2 teaspoon)
ground nutmeg

2 mL (1/2 teaspoon)
ground cinnamon

pinch
salt

1.5 L (6 cups)
apple, peeled and sliced

Method:
To ensure even cooking, you must give the dish or container a half-turn during the cooking period. In order to know when and how often to do this, find a recipe similar to the one you are adapting and follow the instructions given for this procedure.

— Combine the flour and salt. Use a pastry blender to cut the shortening and butter into the flour until the mixture resembles coarse crumbs.
— **Add the food coloring to the water.** Add the water gradually, stirring constantly with a fork until the dough forms a stiff lump.
— Flatten the pastry until it is 1.25 cm (1/2 inch) thick and then, with a rolling pin, roll the pastry out to form a circle 4 mm (1/8 inch) thick.
— Place on a 22.5 cm (9 inch) pie plate, making sure that the pastry extends 2.5 cm (1 inch) over the edge all around.
— Trim the edge to 1.25 cm (1/2 inch).
— **Fold the edge over on itself. Set the leftover pastry aside.**
— **Cook in the microwave oven at 70% for 6 to 7 minutes, giving the plate a half-turn after 3 minutes. Allow to cool.**
— **Use a pastry cutter to cut shapes from the leftover pastry. Arrange on a sheet of waxed paper and cook at 90% for 2 to 4 minutes, giving the pastry a half-turn after 2 minutes. Set aside.**
— Put all the filling ingredients except the apple slices into a bowl and mix. Add the apple and mix again, thoroughly. Spoon the filling into the pie crust.
— **Place a sheet of waxed paper on the floor of the microwave oven. Cook the pie at 70% for 6 to 8 minutes, or until the apple is tender. Give the plate a half-turn after 3 minutes.**
— **Decorate the pie with the cooked pastry shapes.**

Utensils:
Never use any bowl or container that is made of metal or has a metal trim in the microwave oven. However, you can use bowls, dishes and plates made of heat-resistant glass or plastic. You probably have a wide range of suitable containers in your kitchen cupboards and should therefore check to see if you have the right one for a given recipe before buying a new one for that specific purpose.

Cooking Utensils

Cooking is an art that makes use of science and technology in order to produce great tasting food. The scientific and technological aspects of cooking have been developing over many years and include food chemistry and cooking technology. The invention of the microwave oven has brought with it a range of new techniques. Nevertheless, the basic techniques have stayed the same.

For example—and this statement applies not only to baking but to other types of cooking as well—the introduction of the microwave oven has not made traditional cooking utensils obsolete. However, some precautions are required when using them.

This section of the book deals with the utensils most commonly used in baking and bread making. You are probably familiar with most of them, but the following information provides some useful reminders.

Utensils for Measuring
Successful cooking depends on accuracy in measuring ingredients. If the proportions are not right, a dish can be completely ruined. For example, just a little too much liquid in a frosting can ruin the appearance of a cake that is perfect in all other respects. So it is very important to have good equipment for measuring both liquid and dry ingredients. The following are indispensable.

Standard measuring spoons are a must. Do not use ordinary spoons to measure ingredients, as they are rarely accurate. Because Canada was slow to convert to the metric system, many Canadian cookbooks use imperial measures. It is therefore a good idea to have two sets of measuring spoons—one, metric (the international system) and the other, imperial (tablespoon and teaspoon are typical imperial measures). These spoons can be used for both liquid and dry ingredients.

Larger quantities of liquid ingredients are best measured in measuring cups made of glass or some other transparent material. Choose cups that have both metric and imperial measurements. For measuring dry ingredients, it is best to use a set of standard measuring cups that give an accurate measure when filled to the brim. It goes without saying that ordinary cups should never be used for measuring ingredients because they vary so much in size—one cup might hold half again as much as another.

Utensils for Mixing
This category includes sieves, mixers, rolling pins and a host of other gadgets for mixing, shaping and cutting. It is useful to have two sieves: a large one for large amounts of flour and a small one for sieving small amounts of dry ingredients into small containers.

An electric mixer is the modern equivalent of the traditional whisk. This appliance is particularly useful for blending such ingredients as cake mixtures, which must be completely smooth.

The importance of a rolling pin is obvious. Although some people like to use a special cloth cover over it, this is not really necessary. However, professional pastry cooks do recommend the use of a marble work surface for rolling out pastry. Marble is cool and smooth, which makes the pastry easier to work with. If you make pastry often, you would be wise to invest in one.

Don't forget the importance of spatulas. They are useful both for mixing and for transferring mixtures from one bowl or dish to another.

A pastry knife is indispensable for spreading frosting on cakes. It is oblong and has two straight, blunt sides. It is also useful for leveling ingredients in measuring cups.

Baking Pans and Dishes

Any non-metallic baking pan or dish is suitable for use in the microwave oven. However, we recommend that you use round dishes whenever possible. Microwave energy is distributed in such a way that food in the corners of square or rectangular dishes tends to cook more quickly than food in the center. We recommend that you use dishes of transparent glass for cooking pie crusts and cakes because they allow you to check for doneness by a simple visual inspection.

As you can see, microwave cooking does not require that you buy a whole new set of utensils. You probably already have everything you need; thus, you can get right on with baking—and enjoying the results of your work.

Measuring Ingredients

A. Measuring ingredients accurately is a vital first step in successful cooking. It is particularly important in the case of cakes, pastries and other desserts. If you use the wrong amount of such basic and important ingredients as yeast, flour or even salt, the results can be disastrous. However, the use of a few simple techniques will enable you to achieve excellent results. For example, for liquid ingredients a measuring cup must be transparent and have a proper rim and a pouring lip if it is to be accurate. Another way of checking that you have the right quantity is to put the cup on a flat surface and check at eye level that the liquid is right on the mark.

Liquid ingredients used in desserts generally serve to dissolve sugar, salt and yeast in order to activate the starch present in flour. In some cases they add flavor or nutritional value. To measure them accurately, put the measuring cup on a flat surface and check at eye level that the liquid is right on the mark.

MICROTIPS

To Shell Nuts

The microwave oven enables you to shell Brazil nuts, walnuts, almonds and pecans easily. Simply pour 250 mL (1 cup) nuts into a large bowl and cover with 250 mL (1 cup) water. Cover and heat at 100% for 3 to 4 minutes, or until the water reaches boiling point. Allow to stand for 1 minute and then pour the water off. Arrange the nuts on paper towel and leave to cool. Using a nutcracker, shell the nuts but be careful of being burned by any hot water that may still be inside the shell.

B. The use of honey in baking dates back to antiquity. As with syrup or molasses, it makes baked goods—and particularly cookies—sweeter, darker and more strongly flavored. Recipes that call for these ingredients can only be made successfully if you know how to measure them accurately.

It is the stickiness of these ingredients that makes them difficult to measure. For greater accuracy, lightly grease the inside of the measuring cup before adding them.

Grease the sides of the measuring cup to prevent sweet liquids such as honey, molasses and syrup from sticking to them. This step will ensure that the amount you pour and the amount you measure are the same.

C. The main dry ingredients used in desserts are flour, sugar, yeast, baking powder and baking soda. For accurate results, measure these ingredients with proper measuring spoons or cups. An easy way to ensure accuracy is to heap the measure and then level it off with a knife.

Brown sugar must be packed down for measuring. Note the difference in volume between 125 mL (1/2 cup) of brown sugar that has been packed down and the same amount that has not. All the recipes in this volume that call for brown sugar require that it be packed down for measuring.

Eggs are available in different sizes: small, medium, large and extra large. The recipes in this volume require the use of large eggs. If you use a different size, you will have to adapt the recipe accordingly. One large egg measures 50 mL (1/4 cup).

Have you ever had difficulty measuring fat, lard or shortening? Here is a technique, based on a very simple principle, for measuring the right quantity accurately. First pour 125 mL (1/2 cup) cold water into a measuring cup.

Add enough fat to make the water level rise by the desired amount; for example, if you wish to measure 50 mL (1/4 cup) fat in 125 mL (1/2 cup) water, you must add sufficient fat to make the water level rise to 175 mL (3/4 cup).

When you have measured the right amount, pour the water into another container.

Basic Ingredients

Sugar

Sugar is an essential source of energy. The types of sugars found in fruit are simple sugars: glucose, fructose and galactose. The types of sugar used in cooking, particularly in baking and dessert making, have undergone a special manufacturing process. There are five common varieties: white granulated sugar, icing sugar, fruit sugar and brown sugar, which may be refined or unrefined. It is recommended that you use the type of sugar specified in the recipe and do not substitute syrup, molasses or honey.

Flour

Flour is a basic ingredient in dessert making. It is made from ground wheat or other types of grain. Wheat flour is the most common. There are five common varieties: all-purpose flour, enriched flour, pastry flour, cake flour and self-raising flour. All-purpose flour contains the highest proportion of vitamins—those present in the original grain and not destroyed by the milling process—of all the flours. Enriched flour can be used in the same way as all-purpose flour. The only difference is that it contains added minerals and vitamins. Pastry flour is suitable for cakes and pastries and may be used as a substitute for all-purpose flour if baking powder and salt are added to it. Cake flour is very soft, consists only of the wheat starch and can only be used for cakes and some cookies. Finally, self-raising flour is a type of pastry flour to which salt and two types of raising agents, baking soda and baking powder, have been added. If you use it, omit the salt and raising agents specified in the recipe. Unless otherwise specified, the flour required in the recipes throughout this volume is all-purpose flour.

Several types of sugar are available: candy sugar, dark brown sugar, light brown sugar, refined and unrefined. You can substitute one type for another. Bear in mind, however, that dark brown sugar requires a longer cooking time.

Several types of flour are also available. You can substitute a mixture of pastry flour, salt and baking powder for all-purpose flour. For details, consult the chart on page 73.

Raising Agents

Raising agents cause dough or batter to rise. When raising agents are mixed with other ingredients, they give off a colorless, odorless gas that makes the mixture rise. Five types are commonly used: fresh yeast, active dried yeast, baking powder, baking soda and cream of tartar.

Fresh yeast can be bought in small packages from the dairy section of the larger supermarkets. It must be used within a week. Active dried yeast can be obtained in handy individual packages or more economical tins. It keeps for a longer period and gives excellent results. Baking soda, baking powder and cream of tartar are all important raising agents that take effect during the actual

cooking. Baking soda is a chemical raising agent that is frequently used in breads and cakes that contain fruit or chocolate. Baking powder is another type of chemical raising agent often used in quick breads and cakes. Note that it doesn't keep for more than a year. Cream of tartar is sometimes used in conjunction with baking soda, but most frequently to increase the volume of beaten egg whites.

Cookies

Should simplicity be your guide? The answer is surely yes when the subject is cookies, which are made from simple ingredients.

In many cases it takes less than an hour to transform flour, sugar, butter and eggs into delicious cookies. Some cookies are crisp; others have a melt-in-the-mouth texture. You can leave them plain or add fancy toppings, such as almonds or chocolate.

Cookies are very versatile. They can be eaten at your leisure or when you're on the run, at coffee time, at snack time or for dessert. They are a real boon to have on hand for children, for guests . . . and for yourself. Everyone likes cookies.

Your cookie mixture may be one of three possible types: a firm dough, a soft dough or a batter. A very wide selection of ready-made cookies is available, but none can compare with the ones you make yourself. And the microwave oven enables you to make them in less time than it takes to heat a conventional oven. Baking cookies in the microwave is also a great energy saver.

Cookies can be made successfully, even by the novice cook, and there is no limit to the ways in which recipes can be varied to suit your own taste.

In the following pages we present basic techniques for making cookies, techniques that will enable you to make your own personal adaptations.

Basic Methods for Cookies

In days gone by, cookies were either baked in two stages or in a special double-sided pan, something like a waffle iron. People are too busy for such special techniques nowadays and the method for making cookies is much simpler.

To make cookies successfully, it is important to use a flat-bottomed dish. There are cookie sheets and trays especially designed for the microwave oven, but a pie plate made from heat-resistant glass is also suitable.

Avoid dishes that have high sides as they make it difficult to handle the cookies. You will also find it helpful to use a lifter for handling cookies.

When you prepare cookies for baking, arrange them in a circle around the outside of the baking tray and leave 2.5 cm (1 inch) between each. The circle arrangement is very important in ensuring even cooking because microwave energy is concentrated around the outside edges of the tray.

For the same reason, do not have any cookies at the center of the oven because that is where cooking is the slowest.

You can bake between six and nine cookies in the microwave at one time. Always follow the instructions given in the recipe very carefully to obtain successful results. The tray should be raised on a rack in the oven, and the cooking time should be divided into two periods so that you can give the dish a half-turn between each one. Otherwise, the cookies will be unevenly cooked.

It is easy to vary the crispness of your cookies. Some people like their cookies really crisp while others prefer them softer and more moist. You do not have to alter the ingredient proportions to get the result you want; the difference depends on the way in which you bake the cookies.

A. *In a conventional oven the heat causes cookies to brown on the outside.*

B. *Microwaves do not work in the same way as heat. They cook food evenly throughout and do not brown it, so cookies stay pale.*

C. *It is therefore a good idea to make cookies that look appetizing without conventional browning. Alternative approaches are to add food coloring to the cookies, to frost them, or to sprinkle them with colored sugar.*

MICROTIPS

To Soften Brown Sugar

The microwave oven provides the perfect way to deal with brown sugar that has hardened into a solid block. Simply put the block of sugar into a thick plastic bag and add a little water or a quarter of an apple. Tie a piece of string loosely around the opening. Heat at 100% for 20 seconds and check to see if the sugar has softened. Repeat once or twice as necessary, taking care not to let the sugar melt. When it has softened sufficiently take it out of the oven and allow it to stand for 5 minutes. If your block of sugar is small (less than 225 g/ 8 ounces), follow the same procedure but check the sugar every 15 seconds.

If you like your cookies moist, place a sheet of waxed paper over the bottom of the tray in which you bake them. Waxed paper absorbs only a little fat and moisture from the dough.

If you prefer your cookies crisp and drier, bake them on a sheet of paper towel, which absorbs more fat and moisture.

This technique makes it easy to produce cookies to suit everyone in the family. There is nothing to stop you from making one batch of soft cookies on waxed paper and another, crisper batch on paper towel.

Cookies bake very quickly in the microwave oven, usually requiring less than five minutes. As a result, leaving them in even a minute too long can lead to disappointing results. As a precaution against overcooking the recipes give minimum cooking times, and you should follow them closely. However, in some cases (such as when you make larger cookies or use a dough with more liquid) you may have to increase the cooking time a little.

Bake the cookies until the surface is dry, but no longer. Always beware of overcooking, which will cause the cookies to dry out. You can test the cookies for doneness by inserting a toothpick into the center of each. If it does not come out clean let them

cook a little longer. The recipes in this book instruct you to let the cookies stand on the tray for a short time before removing them. This standing time is essential, as it allows the cooking process to finish properly. Also, the cookies will be easier to remove after they have been allowed to stand.

MICROTIPS

How to Make Your Cookies Golden

If cookies baked in the microwave do not turn out as golden as you would like them, try making them with brown sugar instead of white. Their cooking time should then be a little longer than that given in the recipe. Another way to make cookies darker is to use whole wheat flour in place of white.

Chocolate Chip Cookies

Level of Difficulty	🍴
Preparation Time	15 min
Cost per Serving	$
Yield	3 dozen
Cooking Time	4 min per batch
Standing Time	2 min
Power Level	70%
Write Your Cooking Time Here	

Ingredients
125 mL (1/2 cup) butter
150 mL (2/3 cup) brown sugar
1 egg
5 mL (1 teaspoon) vanilla
375 mL (1-1/2 cups) flour
2 mL (1/2 teaspoon) salt
5 mL (1 teaspoon) baking soda
175 mL (3/4 cup) chocolate chips

Method
— Cream the butter. Add the brown sugar gradually, beating constantly, until the mixture is smooth and creamy.
— Stir in the egg and vanilla.
— Combine the flour, salt and baking soda in another bowl. Stir into the butter, sugar and egg mixture. Add the chocolate chips.
— Arrange teaspoonfuls (5 mL) of dough in a circle on a greased baking tray.
— Place the tray on a rack in the oven and cook at 70% for 2 minutes. Give the tray a half-turn and cook for a further 2 minutes.
— Allow to stand for 2 minutes before serving.
— Cook the remaining mixture in the same way.

Begin by assembling all the ingredients required to make these cookies. They are quick and easy to make and are quite delicious.

Use a spatula to cream the butter. Then add the brown sugar gradually, beating all the time, until the mixture is smooth and creamy.

Stir the dry ingredients into the liquid ingredients. Grease a suitable tray and arrange teaspoonfuls (5 mL) of the mixture in a circle around the outside edge.

MICROTIPS

To Coat with Chocolate

Chocolate chips can be used in more things than just cookies. Melt chocolate chips at 50% for 2 to 4 minutes. When the chocolate is completely melted, dip in fruit or cookies in order to cover them entirely. Allow the coating to dry before serving.

Old Fashioned Raisin Cookies

Level of Difficulty	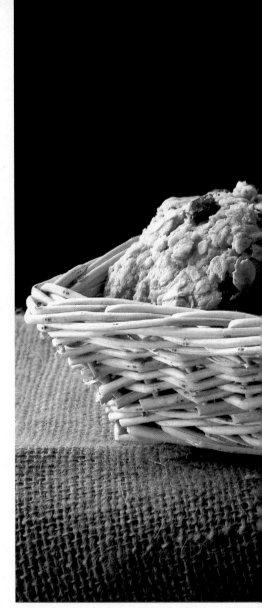
Preparation Time	15 min
Cost per Serving	$ $
Yield	3 dozen
Cooking Time	3 to 4 min per batch
Standing Time	2 min
Power Level	100%, 70%
Write Your Cooking Time Here	

Ingredients
175 mL (3/4 cup) orange juice
250 mL (1 cup) raisins
125 mL (1/2 cup) shortening
175 mL (3/4 cup) sugar
50 mL (1/4 cup) molasses
15 mL (1 tablespoon) orange zest
5 mL (1 teaspoon) vanilla
250 mL (1 cup) quick-cooking oats
5 mL (1 teaspoon) baking powder
5 mL (1 teaspoon) baking soda
5 mL (1 teaspoon) salt
5 mL (1 teaspoon) cinnamon
1 mL (1/4 teaspoon) cloves
625 mL (2-1/2 cups) flour

Method
— Mix the orange juice and the raisins. Heat at 100% for 2 to 3 minutes to bring the liquid to the boiling point. Allow to cool for 10 minutes.
— Combine all the dry ingredients except the sugar and set aside.
— Cream the shortening and slowly blend in the sugar. Mix well.
— Add the molasses and orange zest and then the orange juice and raisins and the vanilla. Mix well.
— Gradually stir in the dry ingredients and mix well until smooth.
— Arrange spoonfuls of the mixture in a circle on a greased tray.
— Place the tray on a rack in the oven and cook at 70% for 2 minutes.
— Give the tray a half-turn and cook at 70% for a further 2 minutes.
— Cook the remaining mixture in the same way.
— Allow to stand for 2 minutes.

MICROTIPS

To Make Cookies Successfully

Most cookies are made of rich dough, which often causes them to cook too quickly. To avoid overcooking, take them out of the oven as soon as the dough begins to thicken. Otherwise the center of the cookies will become hard and dry.

Frozen cookies and cookie mixes from supermarkets do not always produce good results when cooked in microwave ovens. The dough does not cook well. Prepare cookies yourself according to recipes in this book to achieve the best results.

Pour the orange juice into a heat-resistant glass container. Add the raisins. Heat at 100% for 2 to 3 minutes to bring the liquid to the boiling point.

Breads

Bread has been a staple food for mankind since time immemorial. A true yeast bread is made from flour, salt, water and a leavening agent. The dough is kneaded and then shaped or put into pans and baked in the oven.

It is generally thought that the ancient Egyptians discovered the secret of making leavened bread. The discovery spread quickly to all the Mediterranean countries. The Gauls, whom the Romans considered barbarians, made their bread with barley beer and it was deservedly famous.

Bread making became a trade in its own right during the Middle Ages, and the number of different kinds of bread increased dramatically. Although it would take too long to list them all, it is perhaps worth mentioning that the famous French encyclopedia of cooking produced by Larousse names twenty-two kinds. In addition, there are countless regional variations.

It is hardly surprising that there are so many types of bread. It is served in its own right at every meal and is the basic ingredient in crumb coatings, some puddings and croûtons as well. In the case of canapés and sandwiches, bread becomes an edible platter, which holds other types of food.

Because bread is such a staple part of our diet, it is frequently used as a synonym for food itself. "Daily bread" and "breadwinner" are only a couple of examples. You can probably think of many others.

Traditional bread making involves a number of basic procedures, which are followed even when making bread to be cooked in the microwave oven.

The first of these procedures is *kneading*. Kneading blends water, yeast, flour and salt into a smooth dough.

Next, the kneaded dough is *left to rise*. The carbon dioxide given off by the yeast creates air bubbles in the dough and so makes it lighter. The action of the yeast at this stage is what gives bread its unique texture and aroma.

The final stage is *cooking*. Purists cook their bread in wood ovens, but you can achieve perfectly good results in the microwave.

There are several advantages to making your own bread. For one thing, you can ensure that only quality ingredients are used. For another, you can adapt your recipes to suit your menus. For example, you might add nuts, raisins or even bacon bits to a basic bread dough, depending on the type of dish to be served with it.

So don't be put off by the technicalities of using a microwave. The important thing is to produce great tasting bread!

Basic Methods for Bread

Mix the yeast with the liquid (water, milk or a mixture of the two) then add the butter, salt and flour until the dough is quite smooth. Knead the dough for 5 to 6 minutes and shape into a ball. Grease the inside of a transparent bowl and put the dough in it. Brush a little oil over the top of the dough.

Place the bowl containing the dough in a large container filled with hot water, cover with waxed paper and put into the microwave for 25 to 30 minutes at 10%. To test if the dough is sufficiently well risen press the surface gently with two fingers. If the indentations remain, the dough is ready for kneading.

First, use your fist to knock down the dough.

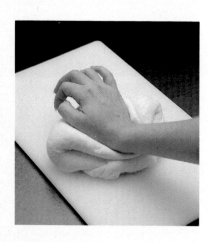

Knead the dough for 5 or 6 minutes and then shape it. Sprinkle it with your choice of topping.

Put the dough into a baking pan. We recommend the use of the traditional rectangular loaf pan or a ring pan for best results.

Don't forget that the dough has to rise a second time. Place the pan in a dish of hot water and put into the microwave at 10% for another 25 to 30 minutes. Turn the dish halfway through this period.

The dough should double in volume. Cook immediately.

To ensure that the bread cooks thoroughly and evenly, place the pan on an upturned saucer. Cook for 6 minutes at 70%. Turn the pan halfway through the cooking time.

To test for doneness, insert a toothpick halfway between the center and the edge of the loaf. If it comes out clean, the bread is done. If it doesn't, cook at 70% for 1 minute or 1 minute 30 seconds longer. Allow to stand and cool before turning out of the pan.

MICROTIPS

To Make Bread Successfully

Here are some practical tips for making successful yeast bread.

Add a little sweetener to the mixture of yeast and warm water to speed up the action of the yeast and to improve the taste. White sugar, molasses, brown sugar and honey are all suitable.

Make sure that the water you use is between 41° C and 46° C (105° F and 115° F). Water that is too hot will kill the yeast and consequently the dough will not rise.

For best results, use as little flour as possible. It is not necessary to use the entire quantity suggested in the recipe. Add just enough to prevent the dough from being sticky. It should still be very soft.

The surrounding temperature affects the time it takes for the dough to rise. In a warm place, two hours will be sufficient. Bear in mind, however, that dough that is allowed to rise slowly has a better flavor. For best results, leave the dough in a cool place for 4 to 5 hours or all night in the refrigerator.

Whole Wheat Bread

Ingredients
1.375 L (5-1/2 cups) warm water
15 mL (1 tablespoon) sea salt
45 mL (3 tablespoons) molasses

45 mL (3 tablespoons) sunflower oil
2 L (8 cups) stone-ground whole wheat flour
30 mL (2 tablespoons) dried yeast

30 mL (2 tablespoons) raised yeast, available in supermarkets

Method
— Mix the water with the salt, molasses and sunflower oil. Set aside.
— Mix the two types of yeast and add the flour, mix well.
— Begin by mixing 500 mL to 1 L (2 to 4 cups) flour into the liquid mixture. Add the remaining flour gradually, mixing until the dough comes away from the sides of the bowl.
— Knead gently for 6 to 10 minutes.
— Shape into 4 loaves and place in greased pans of heat-resistant glass.
— Brush a little oil over the tops of the loaves.
— Cover with a damp cloth. Allow to stand until the loaves have doubled in volume.
— Place on a rack in the microwave oven and cook

Level of Difficulty	🍴
Preparation Time	40 min
Cost per Serving	$ $
Yield	4 loaves
Cooking Time	6 min per loaf
Standing Time	10 min
Power Level	70%
Write Your Cooking Time Here	

This chart applies to the recipes on pages 32 and 33.

Poppy Seed Bread

Ingredients

500 mL (2 cups) warm 2%
milk
500 mL (2 cups) warm water
75 mL (1/3 cup) sunflower
oil
15 mL (1 tablespoon) salt
30 mL (2 tablespoons) sugar
1.75 to 2 L (7 to 8 cups)
flour
40 mL (2 rounded
tablespoons) dried yeast
125 mL (1/2 cup) poppy
seeds

Method

— Dissolve the yeast and
  sugar in 125 mL (1/2 cup)
  warm water. Leave for 10
  minutes.
— In a large bowl combine
  the milk, the remainder of
  the water, the oil and salt.
— Stir in 1 L (4 cups) flour
  and mix well.
— Add the yeast mixture and
  then the poppy seeds,
  reserving some poppy
  seeds to sprinkle on top of
  the loaves.
— Stir well until the mixture
  is smooth.
— Add the remaining flour
  gradually, mixing until the
  dough comes away from
  the sides of the bowl.
— Place the dough on a
  floured surface and knead
  for 6 to 8 minutes.
— Divide the dough into 4
  and shape into loaves.
— Grease 4 pans and place a
  loaf in each.
— Brush a little oil over the
  top of each loaf. Cover
  with a damp cloth and
  leave to rise until doubled
  in volume. Sprinkle with
  the remaining poppy
  seeds.
— Cook each loaf separately
  at 70% for 3 minutes.
  Raise the pan on an
  upturned saucer when
  cooking.
— Give the pan a half-turn
  and continue cooking at
  70% for another 3
  minutes.

each loaf separately at
70% for 3 minutes. Give
the loaves a half-turn and
continue to cook for
another 3 minutes at 70%.
Test for doneness by
inserting a toothpick
halfway between the
center and the edge of the
loaf. If the toothpick does
not come out clean,
continue to cook until the
bread is done.
— Allow to stand for 10
  minutes on a wire rack
  before slicing.

Whole Wheat Banana Bread

Level of Difficulty	🍴
Preparation Time	10 min
Cost per Serving	$
Yield	1 loaf, approximately 12 servings
Cooking Time	11 min
Standing Time	5 min
Power Level	50%, 100%
Write Your Cooking Time Here	

Ingredients

Bread:
125 mL (1/2 cup) butter
125 mL (1/2 cup) brown sugar
2 eggs
15 mL (1 tablespoon) lemon juice or vinegar
75 mL (1/3 cup) milk
250 mL (1 cup) whole wheat flour
125 mL (1/2 cup) all-purpose flour
2 mL (1/2 teaspoon) salt
5 mL (1 teaspoon) baking soda
2 bananas, mashed
30 mL (2 tablespoons) butter
Topping:
125 mL (1/2 cup) flour
60 mL (4 tablespoons) dark brown sugar
pinch cinnamon
30 mL (2 tablespoons) butter

Method
— Cream 125 mL (1/2 cup) butter.
— Add the brown sugar and mix well. Stir in the eggs. Set aside.
— Stir the lemon juice (or vinegar) into the milk.
— Sift together the two types of flour, salt and baking soda.
— Blend the dry ingredients, alternately with the milk, into the butter, sugar and egg mixture.

— Add the bananas and mix well.
— Grease the loaf pan with 30 mL (2 tablespoons) butter and pour the mixture into the pan.
— Mix the topping ingredients together and sprinkle over the loaf batter.
— Cover the ends of the pan with a 2.5 cm (1 inch)-wide strip of aluminum foil.
— Place on a rack in the oven and cook at 50% for

5 minutes. Turn the pan, remove the foil and cook at 50% for another 4 minutes.
— Raise the power level to 100% and cook for a further 2 minutes.
— Allow to stand for 5 minutes before slicing.

Pour the batter into a rectangular loaf pan. Add the topping and cover the two narrow ends of the pan with aluminum foil.

Cook at 50% for 5 minutes, turn the pan and cook for another 4 minutes at 50%. Increase the power level to 100% and continue to cook for 2 more minutes.

Apple Spice Bread

Level of Difficulty	
Preparation Time	10 min
Cost per Serving	$ $
Yield	1 loaf, approximately 12 servings
Cooking Time	10 min
Standing Time	5 min
Power Level	50%
Write Your Cooking Time Here	

Ingredients
50 mL (1/4 cup) shortening
175 mL (3/4 cup) sugar
2 eggs
175 mL (3/4 cup) applesauce
50 mL (1/4 cup) milk
15 mL (1 tablespoon) lemon juice or vinegar
375 mL (1-1/2 cups) flour
5 mL (1 teaspoon) salt
5 mL (1 teaspoon) baking soda
5 mL (1 teaspoon) cinnamon
1 mL (1/4 teaspoon) nutmeg
1 mL (1/4 teaspoon) cloves
50 mL (1/4 cup) raisins, floured
50 mL (1/4 cup) walnuts

Method
— Cream the shortening and sugar together. Add the eggs and mix well.
— Add the applesauce, milk and lemon juice (or vinegar).
— Sift together the flour, salt, baking soda, cinnamon, nutmeg and cloves. Stir gradually into the liquid mixture.
— Add the raisins and nuts, mix well and pour into a greased loaf pan.
— Cover the two narrow ends of the pan with a 2.5 cm (1 inch)-wide strip of aluminum foil.
— Place on a rack in the oven and cook at 50% for 5 minutes. Remove the aluminum foil, give the pan a half-turn and cook at 50% for another 5 minutes.
— Test for doneness by inserting a toothpick between the center and the edge of the loaf. Cook for a little longer if it does not come out clean.
— Allow to stand for 5 minutes before slicing.

MICROTIPS

To Cook Bread Successfully

Because the microwaves are less intense in the center of the oven, bread placed there may not always cook properly, even in the time specified. This problem can be dealt with simply by putting the bread back into its pan and cooking on a rack at 50% for 2 to 3 minutes. It is easy to correct undercooked bread in this way, but there is nothing you can do with overcooked bread.

Always allow bread to cool before cutting, otherwise it will be too crumbly. Besides, the cooling period allows the flavor to develop. To cool bread, turn it out onto a wire rack so that the air can circulate around it and the excess moisture can evaporate.

Muffins

Muffins, which belong to Anglo-Saxon cooking traditions, are good to eat at any time of the day. They contain many nutritious ingredients, such as flour, oats, bran and wheatgerm, so they are a perfect food to get the day off to a good start. The fact that they are a healthy food does not make them dull; they are sweet enough to serve at afternoon tea or in place of a dessert high in calories.

You can vary the taste and the appearance of your muffins by your choice of ingredients. Fruit (such as dates, raisins or blueberries) and chopped nuts may be added. You can use brown or white flour, sugar or syrup. They may simply be topped with nuts—e.g., chopped almonds. You can even sneak in a few chocolate chips if you wish.

There is no doubt that muffins are very popular. They make wonderful additions to kids' lunches and are greatly appreciated at snack time.

Because muffins have a high fiber content, they belong in any well-balanced diet. However, if you like to indulge your sweet tooth once in a while, you can smother them in syrup or with your favorite spread. Muffins are so versatile that they can be as healthy or as sinful as you like.

We have space in this book for only four muffin recipes, but they provide you with the basic techniques for adapting your own muffin recipes to microwave cooking. Don't forget to check the section on pages 10 and 11 for some of the basic principles on this topic.

Muffins cooked in the microwave oven are just as delicious as those made in the traditional way. The main difference is the speed at which they can be prepared. Cooking is so fast that you can make them at breakfast and still be on time for work.

Basic Methods for Muffins

The cooking times given are correct for muffins of the specified size. Always use large baking cups and fill them two-thirds full. If you put more batter in, they may overflow during cooking and the muffins may be undercooked.

Muffin batter cooks more quickly than any other in the microwave oven. You can have piping hot muffins ready to eat in 5 minutes. Here are some tips on how to make the quickest muffins ever.

— As stated in the recipes, use large baking cups. The cooking time given in each recipe is correct for the amount of batter that will fit comfortably into this size of cup. Cups of a different size will yield results that are not as good.

— Some microwave muffin pans have space for a muffin in the center. Do not use the center compartment. As we have said before, microwave energy is least efficient in the center of the oven and the muffin would not cook properly.

— To ensure even cooking, place the pan on a rack in the oven and turn it halfway through the cooking time.

— Combine all the muffin ingredients in a bowl and stir lightly, until just mixed.

— Fill each cup just two-thirds full to ensure that the batter does not overflow during cooking.

You can decorate your muffins in a variety of different ways. For example, a nut topping is both attractive and appetizing. Muffins topped with sliced almonds or other chopped nuts would go very well with an American-style lunch. Coconut, raisins and dates are other excellent suggestions for toppings that are decorative and delicious.

Chocolate Muffins

Ingredients
175 mL (3/4 cup) milk
1 egg, beaten
50 mL (1/4 cup) oil
250 mL (1 cup) bran
250 mL (1 cup) flour
12 mL (2-1/2 teaspoons) baking powder
2 mL (1/2 teaspoon) salt
45 mL (3 tablespoons) cocoa
125 mL (1/2 cup) sugar
125 mL (1/2 cup) chocolate chips

Method
— Put large baking cups in a microwave-safe muffin pan.
— Combine milk, egg and oil, stir in the bran and set aside for 5 minutes.
— Sift together the flour, baking powder, salt and cocoa.
— Add the sugar to the liquid ingredients and bran, and then stir in the flour mixture.
— Add the chocolate chips and put the batter into the baking cups.
— Place on a rack in the oven and cook at 90% for 2 to 2-1/2 minutes, turning the pan halfway through the cooking time.
— Turn the muffins out of the pan and allow to stand for 3 minutes.
— Cook the remaining batter in the same way.

Level of Difficulty	🍴🍴
Preparation Time	10 min
Cost per Serving	$ $
Yield	18 muffins
Cooking Time	2 to 2-1/2 min per batch
Standing Time	3 min
Power Level	90%
Write Your Cooking Time Here	

Whole Wheat Honey Muffins

Ingredients

425 mL (1-3/4 cups) whole
wheat flour
20 mL (4 teaspoons) baking
powder
2 mL (1/2 teaspoon) salt

1 egg, beaten
175 mL (3/4 cup) milk
75 mL (1/3 cup) honey
50 mL (1/4 cup) oil
75 mL (1/3 cup) chopped
walnuts

Method

— Combine all the dry
  ingredients. In another
  bowl, blend all the liquid
  ingredients together.
— Pour one mixture into the
  other and stir until the
  batter is evenly mixed. It
  will still be a little lumpy.
— Put the batter into large
  baking cups in a
  microwave-safe muffin
  pan. Fill each cup just
  two-thirds full.
— Place on a rack in the
  oven and cook at 90% for
  2-1/2 minutes, turning the
  pan halfway through the
  cooking time.
— Turn the muffins out of
  the pan and allow to stand
  for 3 minutes.
— Cook the remaining batter
  in the same way.

Level of Difficulty	🍴🔪
Preparation Time	10 min
Cost per Serving	$ $
Yield	1 dozen
Cooking Time	2-1/2 min per batch
Standing Time	3 min
Power Level	90%
Write Your Cooking Time Here	

Molasses Bran Muffins

Level of Difficulty	🍴🍴
Preparation Time	10 min
Cost per Serving	$
Yield	1 dozen
Cooking Time	2-1/2 to 3 min per batch
Standing Time	3 min
Power Level	90%
Write Your Cooking Time Here	

Ingredients
5 mL (1 teaspoon) melted margarine
50 mL (1/4 cup) molasses
375 mL (1-1/2 cups) skim milk
1 egg, beaten
375 mL (1-1/2 cups) bran
250 mL (1 cup) flour
10 mL (2 teaspoons) baking powder
5 mL (1 teaspoon) salt

Method
— Arrange large baking cups in a 6-cup microwave-safe muffin pan.
— Blend the margarine, molasses, milk and egg together and stir in the bran. Set aside.
— Sift the flour, salt and baking powder into another bowl.
— Stir the dry ingredients into the liquid ingredients. Fill each baking cup two-thirds full with the batter.
— Place on a rack in the oven and cook at 90% for 2-1/2 to 3 minutes, turning halfway through the cooking time.
— Turn the muffins out of the pan and allow to stand for 3 minutes.
— Cook the remaining batter in the same way.

Date Bran Muffins

Level of Difficulty	🍴
Preparation Time	15 min
Cost per Serving	$ $
Yield	1 dozen
Cooking Time	2 to 2-1/2 min per batch
Standing Time	3 min
Power Level	100%, 90%
Write Your Cooking Time Here	

Ingredients
250 mL (1 cup) milk
250 mL (1 cup) All Bran
250 mL (1 cup) whole wheat flour
5 mL (1 teaspoon) baking powder
2 mL (1/2 teaspoon) salt
50 mL (1/4 cup) butter
125 mL (1/2 cup) brown sugar
1 egg, beaten
75 mL (1/3 cup) chopped nuts
125 mL (1/2 cup) chopped dates

Method
— Pour the milk into a 500 mL (16 oz) cup and add the All Bran. Set aside.
— Sift the flour, baking powder and salt into a bowl.
— Melt the butter in a large bowl at 100% for 45 seconds, and add the brown sugar, egg, All Bran and milk mixture, the sifted flour mixture and the nuts and dates.
— Mix well and put the batter into large baking cups in a microwave-safe muffin pan. Fill each just two-thirds full.
— Place on a rack in the oven and cook at 90% for 2 to 2-1/2 minutes, turning the pan halfway through the cooking time.
— Turn out of the pan and allow to stand for 3 minutes.
— Cook the remaining batter in the same way.

Cakes

Cultural traditions are more than mere rituals; they also invite us to celebrate and to enjoy ourselves. Think of the number of celebrations that have a cake as the traditional centerpiece. The exquisitely decorated cakes made for weddings and christenings are truly works of art. There are simnel cakes at Easter, rich fruit cakes at Christmas and a host of other cakes belonging to different cultural traditions.

Not that anyone need limit their enjoyment of cakes to special occasions. Indeed, some people claim that eating cake is a special occasion in its own right, to be enjoyed with a cup of good coffee or tea. Or, you can go all out and have cake with a glass of wine.

Many cakes popular today are elaborate creations, but cake making actually had very modest beginnings. The earliest cakes were plain, sweetened with just a little honey. They became more elaborate as travel and trade brought new ideas and new ingredients. As early as the fourth century B.C., the Greeks made simple cakes from a mixture of almonds, poppy seeds, honey and black pepper, rolled in a simple flour-based dough. Honey was gradually replaced as a sweetener after sugar cane was discovered. The Crusades brought the Western world into contact with the Arab world and soon such exotic spices as cinnamon, nutmeg, ginger and cloves were enjoyed by Frankish lords and Italian merchants.

The baker's art was revolutionized once again with the discovery of chocolate, brought to Europe in the sixteenth century by the Conquistadors. At the same time, refinements in the milling process produced better flours with finer textures than ever before.

In this book you will find simple recipes for some very popular cakes. You will learn the special techniques required to produce successful cakes in the microwave oven. If you have friends who are skeptical about the use of the microwave, these superb cakes will truly amaze them.

Successful Cake Making

Choosing Pans

A wide range of pans for cake making is available. You can use circular pans (9 inches in diameter), rectangular pans (10 inches by 6 inches) or square pans (8 inches by 8 inches). We recommend that you use round pans made of glass to ensure even cooking and to allow you to check whether or not a cake is done simply by visual inspection. Tube pans (Bundt pans) also give good results. Because the microwaves are less effective in the center of the microwave oven, the use of a tube pan avoids the problem of cakes that are undercooked in the center.

If you use an ordinary square pan, reduce the power by one level.

MICROTIPS

To Make Cakes Successfully

1. If your microwave oven does not have its own turntable, turn your cake several times during the cooking process.

2. Begin your cooking at medium power (50%). Check after 4 or 5 minutes. If your cake seems to be cooking evenly, continue at this power level. If not, reduce the power level and continue to cook, checking regularly for even cooking. Test for doneness by inserting a toothpick in the cake halfway between the center and the sides. If it comes out clean, the cake is done.

3. Allow the cake to cool completely before turning it out of the pan.

Preparing Cake Pans for Use in the Microwave Oven

Cover the bottom of the pan with parchment paper if you wish to turn the cake out and frost it. The parchment stops the cake from sticking to the bottom of the pan and it can therefore be turned out easily.

An alternative is to spray on a non-stick coating, such as Pam. It comes in a handy aerosol spray can and prevents sticking, as does parchment paper.

Another way to ensure that your cake will turn out easily is to grease the pan and then cover it with Graham crumbs. The crumbs also give your cake a lovely golden surface.

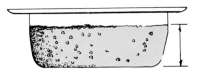

The amount of batter in the pan naturally affects the cooking time. It is recommended that you fill the pan only two-thirds full. If you add too much batter, it will overflow and the cake will be ruined. If, when you have filled the pan two-thirds full, there is still some batter left but not enough to fill another pan, use it up by making cupcakes.

When cooking cakes in the microwave oven, you should always place them on a rack. Even cooking depends on even exposure to the microwaves, which is ensured by using a rack. This allows the microwaves to penetrate the cake from every angle. If you do not have a special rack, place the pan on an upturned saucer.

You should also give the cake pan a half-turn while in the microwave to ensure even cooking. This turning remedies any unevenness in the way the microwaves are distributed in the oven.

If, as we recommend, you use glass pans, you can test for doneness simply by looking at the cake. Take the pan out of the oven and check the bottom. A cake cooked in a round pan is done if there is a circle of uncooked batter about 5 cm (2 inches) in diameter in the center. This will cook during the standing time. A cake cooked in a large tube pan, however, should be completely done because these pans are too deep to allow cooking to continue during the standing time.

You can test for doneness in the traditional way, by inserting a toothpick into the cake. If you are using a tube pan, insert the toothpick near the edge of the pan. If, however, you are using a round, square or rectangular pan, insert the toothpick between the center and the edge. If the toothpick comes out clean, the cake is done. This method is a very reliable test for doneness.

Like all foods, cakes continue to cook during the standing time. Microwave cooking results from the heat provided when the microwaves stimulate the molecules in the food. Also, do not be concerned if the cake is moist on top when it comes out of the oven. This moisture will evaporate as the cake cools, and the surface will be cooked and properly dry.

MICROTIPS

To Make Cakes Rise Properly

Cake batter must be very thoroughly mixed, not only to blend the ingredients well but also to ensure the even distribution of tiny air cells that cause the cake to rise. We also recommend that you let the batter stand for 5 minutes before you put it in the oven. Otherwise, the cake may not rise properly in the center.

Cooking Times for Cupcakes

Quantity	Power Level		
	650/700 watts	600 watts	500 watts
1	25 to 30 s	30 to 45 s	30 to 45 s
2	45 s to 1-1/4 min	1 to 1-1/2 min	1 to 1-1/2 min
3	1 to 1-1/2 min	1-1/4 to 1-3/4 min	1-1/4 to 1-3/4 min
4	1-1/4 to 1-3/4 min	1-3/4 to 2-1/4 min	1-3/4 to 2-1/4 min
5	2 to 2-1/2 min	2-1/2 to 3 min	2-1/2 to 3 min

Practical Tips

To Soften Fat

Shortening and lard can be more easily blended into cake batter if softened. To soften 125 g (4 oz) of fat, heat at 30% for 10 seconds, turning once. To soften 175 g (6 oz) of fat, heat at 30% for 10 to 15 seconds, also turning once.

A Garnish for Cakes

Toasted hazel nuts are a garnish that will enhance even the most basic cakes. Simply spread the hazel nuts on a microwave-safe dish and heat at 100% for 5 minutes, stirring at 1 minute intervals to prevent them from burning.

Food Coloring

It is always wise to measure food coloring into a teaspoon before adding to a batter to prevent the accidental addition of too much. Always mix food coloring very thoroughly into the batter before making the decision to add more.

To Turn a Cake Out of Its Pan

It is much easier to turn a cake out of its pan if you first grease the pan and line it with waxed paper. The waxed paper should extend over the edges of the pan.

Simple Ways to Test if Cakes Are Done

A cake is done if:
— a toothpick inserted between the center and the outside edge of the cake comes out clean.
— the surface of the cake springs back when you press it lightly with your finger.
— the edges of the cake show signs of coming away from the sides of the pan.
— there is a circle of uncooked batter no more than 5 centimetres (2 inches) visible at the bottom of the pan (when you check the bottom of a glass pan).

Freezing Tips

Buns and slices of cake freeze very well. Simply wrap them in plastic film or aluminum foil.

Pineapple Cake

Level of Difficulty	🍴
Preparation Time	20 min
Cost per Serving	$ $
Yield	1 cake, approximately 6 servings
Cooking Time	5 to 7 min
Standing Time	None
Power Level	100%, 70%
Write Your Cooking Time Here	

Ingredients
75 mL (5 tablespoons) butter
175 mL (3/4 cup) brown sugar
4 slices pineapple
4 cherries
250 mL (1 cup) flour
1 mL (1/4 teaspoon) salt
5 mL (1 teaspoon) baking powder
3 egg yolks
250 mL (1 cup) white sugar
90 mL (6 tablespoons) pineapple juice
3 egg whites

Method
— Melt the butter at 100% for 30 to 40 seconds in the cake pan. Sprinkle the brown sugar evenly over the butter. Arrange the pineapple and cherries in the mixture, pressing on them to line the bottom of the pan. Set aside.
— Sift together the flour, salt and baking powder.
— Beat the egg yolks with the white sugar and blend in the flour alternately with the pineapple juice.
— Beat the egg whites until stiff and fold into the batter. Pour onto the pineapple in the cake pan. Place on a rack in the oven and cook at 70% for 5 to 7 minutes. Turn halfway through the cooking time.
— Turn the cake out of the pan as soon as you take it out of the oven.

Assemble all the ingredients required for this pineapple cake, which is sure to satisfy your most demanding guests.

Melt the butter at 100% for 30 to 40 seconds and sprinkle the brown sugar over it, distributing it evenly over the butter in the bottom of the pan.

Arrange the pineapple slices in the mixture on the bottom of the pan. Place a cherry in the center of each slice.

Make a batter with the egg yolks, sugar, sifted flour and pineapple juice. Fold in the stiffly beaten egg whites and pour the batter over the pineapple.

Banana Cake

Ingredients

125 mL (1/2 cup) butter
325 mL (1-1/3 cups) white or
brown sugar
2 egg yolks
500 mL (2 cups) flour
2 mL (1/2 teaspoon) baking
soda
5 mL (1 teaspoon) baking
powder
2 mL (1/2 teaspoon) salt
175 mL (3/4 cup) sour milk
250 mL (1 cup) ripe bananas
(3 or 4), mashed

Method

— Cream the butter with the
  sugar until light and
  fluffy.
— Beat the egg yolks until
  they are thick and pale in
  color and mix well with
  butter and sugar.
— Sift the flour, baking
  soda, baking powder and
  salt together.
— Stir these dry ingredients
  into the butter, sugar and
egg mixture, alternating
with the sour milk and
ending with the dry
ingredients. Add the
bananas.
— Beat the batter until it is
  quite smooth.
— Pour the batter into a
  cake pan. Place on a rack
in the oven and cook at
70% for 10 minutes,
turning halfway through
the cooking time. Increase
the power level to 100%
and cook for a further 2
minutes.
— Allow to stand for 10 to
  15 minutes.

Level of Difficulty	🍴
Preparation Time	15 min
Cost per Serving	$
Yield	1 cake, approximately 12 servings
Cooking Time	12 min
Standing Time	10 to 15 min
Power Level	70%, 100%
Write Your Cooking Time Here	

White Cake

Ingredients
250 mL (1 cup) butter
500 mL (2 cups) sugar
750 mL (3 cups) flour
2 mL (1/2 teaspoon) salt

15 mL (1 tablespoon) baking powder
4 eggs
250 mL (1 cup) milk
10 mL (2 teaspoons) vanilla

Method
— Cream the butter and add the sugar gradually until the mixture becomes fluffy.
— Sift together the flour, salt and baking powder.
— Beat the eggs, one at a time, into the butter and sugar, and then add the flour, alternately with the milk. Begin and end with the flour mixture.
— Add the vanilla, mix well and pour into a tube pan.
— Place on a rack in the oven and cook at 70% for 7 to 9 minutes, turning halfway through the cooking time.
— Allow to stand for 5 to 10 minutes before turning out of the pan.
Note that the surface of the cake will dry out properly during the standing period.

Level of Difficulty	🍴
Preparation Time	20 min
Cost per Serving	$ $
Yield	1 cake, approximately 10 servings
Cooking Time	7 to 9 min
Standing Time	5 to 10 min
Power Level	70%
Write Your Cooking Time Here	

Fruit Cake

Level of Difficulty	⑂⑂
Preparation Time	25 min
Cost per Serving	$ $ $
Yield	1 cake, approximately 12 servings
Cooking Time	10 to 12 min
Standing Time	10 to 15 min
Power Level	50%
Write Your Cooking Time Here	

Ingredients
75 mL (1/3 cup) butter
175 mL (3/4 cup) brown sugar
1 egg
85 g (3 oz) candied fruit
85 g (3 oz) glacé cherries
375 mL (1-1/2 cups) flour
2 mL (1/2 teaspoon) baking soda
7 mL (1-1/2 teaspoons) baking powder
75 mL (1/3 cup) milk
175 mL (3/4 cup) sultana raisins
85 g (3 oz) walnuts

Method
— Cream the butter with the brown sugar. Add the egg and beat well. Stir in the candied fruit and glacé cherries.
— Sift together the flour, baking soda and baking powder.
— Add the flour mixture, alternately with the milk, to the butter, sugar and egg mixture. Begin and end with the dry ingredients.
— Coat the raisins with a little flour. Add to the batter along with the nuts.
— Put the batter into a loaf pan, cover the cake with plastic wrap, leaving a small opening and then cover the ends of the pan with a wide strip of aluminum foil. Place on a rack or on an upturned plate in the oven.
— Cook at 50% for 5 minutes and then remove the aluminum foil and plastic wrap.
— Give the pan a half-turn and continue to cook for another 5 minutes at 50%.
— Insert a toothpick into the cake between the center and the outside edge to test for doneness. Cook for a little longer if necessary.
— Allow to stand for 10 to 15 minutes on a wire rack.

Assemble all the ingredients required for the fruit cake. This traditional dessert will delight your guests.

Cover the loaf pan with plastic wrap, leaving one side open. Then cover the ends of the pan with aluminum foil.

Place on a rack or on an upturned plate to cook. Cook at 50% for 5 minutes, remove the aluminum foil and plastic wrap and then cook for a further 5 minutes.

Cheesecake

Level of Difficulty	![cutlery icon]
Preparation Time	20 min
Cost per Serving	$ $
Yield	1 cake, approximately 10 servings
Cooking Time	3 min
Standing Time	6 to 8 hr in the refrigerator
Power Level	100%, 70%, 30%
Write Your Cooking Time Here	

Ingredients

Crust:
125 mL (1/2 cup) butter
250 mL (1 cup) Graham crumbs
5 mL (1 teaspoon) cinnamon

Filling:
225 g (8 oz) cream cheese
250 mL (1 cup) 35% cream
7 mL (1-1/2 teaspoons) vanilla
250 mL (1 cup) icing sugar
1 envelope unflavored gelatin (optional)

Method

— Melt the butter at 100% for 60 to 90 seconds. Add the Graham crumbs and cinnamon and mix thoroughly.
— Grease a round pan with straight sides. Arrange two strips of plastic wrap crosswise over the bottom of the pan. The strips should be long enough to extend over the sides of the pan so you can use them to lift the cheesecake out.
— Line the bottom with a round of waxed paper. Put the crumb mixture into the pan and spread it evenly.
— Place on a rack in the oven and cook at 70% for 3 minutes, and then set aside to cool.
— Prepare the filling. First soften the cheese by heating at 30% for 45 to 60 seconds. Add the cream and mix well.
— Stir in the vanilla and add the icing sugar gradually. For a firmer texture, dissolve the contents of one envelope of gelatin in water and add to the cheese mixture.
— Spoon the mixture into the crust and refrigerate for 6 to 8 hours. Top with the fruit glaze of your choice.

MICROTIPS

To Make a Cake From A Mix

Cake mixes from supermarkets are not always baked the same way in microwaves as in conventional ovens. Replace 75 mL (1/3 cup) liquid with 75 mL (1/3 cup) oil. If the cake mix requires 2 eggs, use only one. Finally, if it recommends reducing the amount of water, do not.

Arrange two strips of plastic wrap crosswise over the bottom of the pan and line the bottom with a round of waxed paper so that the cheesecake will be easy to lift out.

Put the mixture of butter, Graham crumbs and cinnamon into the pan and spread it evenly. Cook at 70 % for 3 minutes and set aside.

Strawberry Shortcake

Level of Difficulty	🍴
Preparation Time	30 min
Cost per Serving	$ $
Yield	1 2-layer cake, approximately 8 servings
Cooking Time	5 to 6 min per layer
Standing Time	
Power Level	70%
Write Your Cooking Time Here	

Ingredients
5 eggs
250 mL (1 cup) flour
pinch salt
5 mL (1 teaspoon) baking powder
250 mL (1 cup) sugar
50 mL (1/4 cup) vegetable oil
5 mL (1 teaspoon) lemon extract
strawberries, according to taste
35% cream, whipped, according to taste

Method
— Separate the egg yolks from the whites.
— Sift together the flour, salt and baking powder.
— Beat the egg whites until stiff, gradually adding the sugar after they have become foamy.
— In another bowl, beat the egg yolks. Stir into the egg whites.
— Beat continuously as you gradually add the oil, then the sifted flour and lemon extract.
— Line the bottoms of 2 round straight-edged pans with waxed paper.
— Pour half the mixture into each pan. Cook each layer separately.
— Place on a rack in the oven and cook at 70% for 3 minutes.
— Give the pan a half-turn and cook at 70% for a further 2 to 3 minutes. Test for doneness by inserting a toothpick into the cake. Cook for a little longer if necessary.
— Allow the layers to cool completely on a wire rack before sandwiching together and decorating with whipped cream and strawberries.

Queen Elizabeth Cake

Level of Difficulty	🍴🍴
Preparation Time	25 min
Cost per Serving	$ $
Yield	1 cake, approximately 15 servings
Cooking Time	16 to 18 min
Standing Time	5 to 10 min
Power Level	100%, 70%
Write Your Cooking Time Here	

Ingredients
250 mL (1 cup) dates
250 mL (1 cup) hot water
50 mL (1/4 cup) butter
250 mL (1 cup) sugar
2 eggs, beaten
5 mL (1 teaspoon) vanilla
375 mL (1-1/2 cups) flour
5 mL (1 teaspoon) baking soda
5 mL (1 teaspoon) baking powder

Caramel Sauce:
250 mL (1 cup) brown sugar
250 mL (1 cup) flaked coconut
60 mL (4 tablespoons) 35% cream
150 mL (2/3 cup) butter

Method
— Boil the dates in the hot water at 100% for 3 to 4 minutes. Mix to a smooth purée and leave to cool for 10 to 15 minutes.
— Cream the butter, gradually add the sugar and mix well. Stir in the beaten eggs and the vanilla.
— Sift together the flour, baking soda and baking powder.
— Beat the dry ingredients into the butter mixture and then add the date purée.
— Spray Pam on the inside of a tube pan and pour in the batter, place on a rack in the oven and cook at 70% for 5 minutes.
— Give the pan a half-turn and continue to cook at 70% for another 5 minutes.
— Test for doneness by inserting a toothpick and continue to cook if necessary. Let stand for 5 to 10 minutes to cool.

— Prepare the caramel sauce by mixing the brown sugar, flaked coconut, cream and butter well. Boil the mixture at 100% for 3 to 4 minutes. Spread over the cake and reheat for 40 to 60 seconds before serving.

Coat the base and sides of the pan with Pam, pour in the batter, place on a rack in the oven and cook at 70% for 5 minutes. Give the pan a half-turn and cook for another 5 minutes.

Turn the cake out of the pan when it has cooled. Cover with caramel sauce and reheat for 40 to 60 seconds before serving.

Chocolate Fudge Cake

Level of Difficulty	(utensils icon)
Preparation Time	20 min
Cost per Serving	$ $
Yield	1 cake, approximately 10 servings
Cooking Time	8 min per layer
Standing Time	5 to 10 min
Power Level	70%
Write Your Cooking Time Here	(apple and pencil icon)

Ingredients
125 mL (1/2 cup) butter
500 mL (2 cups) sugar
5 mL (1 teaspoon) vanilla
2 eggs
650 mL (2-2/3 cups) flour
2 mL (1/2 teaspoon) salt
10 mL (2 teaspoons) baking soda
125 mL (1/2 cup) cocoa
500 mL (2 cups) sour milk

Method
— Cream the butter and gradually add the sugar and vanilla. Beat until the mixture is light and fluffy.
— Beat the eggs and add to the butter mixture.
— Sift the flour, salt, baking soda and cocoa together 4 or 5 times.
— Add the dry ingredients, alternately with the milk, to the butter mixture. Begin and end with the dry ingredients.
— Line the bottoms of 2 round pans with waxed paper and pour half the batter into each.
— Cook each layer separately. Place on a rack in the oven and cook at 70% for 4 minutes. Give the pan a half-turn and cook at 70% for a further 4 minutes. Test for doneness by inserting a toothpick. Cook for a little longer if it does not come out clean.
— Cook the other layer in the same way.
— Allow to stand for 5 to 10 minutes on a wire rack before turning out of the pan.
— When cool, ice with frosting of your choice.

MICROTIPS

For Even Cooking

Although round pans are best for baking cakes, square or rectangular pans can be used. Because microwave energy is more intense around the edges, it is important to slow the rate of cooking at these points. You can do so by shielding the corners with aluminum foil.

Frostings

The frosting chosen to complement a cake is its crowning touch. There are almost as many types of frostings as there are cakes and they provide a luxurious finish.

The frosting should complement a cake in both color and flavor. This of course is, to a large extent, a matter of personal taste: some people cannot imagine a chocolate cake with anything but a chocolate frosting; others find a contrasting icing more enticing.

Most cooks are familiar with simple frostings made from icing sugar and water. This type of frosting dries to a lovely, satin finish. Although cakes cooked in the microwave are every bit as delicious as cakes cooked in the conventional way, it is true that they remain pale and frosting is the perfect way to improve their appearance.

More elaborate frostings, such as meringues, can also be used. This volume is meant to offer simple, more basic recipes.

The creamy texture, subtle flavor and tempting appearance of frosting is a tribute to your skill as a cook and your pride as a host or hostess. Your guests are sure to appreciate your efforts and some will pay the added tribute of requesting a second helping.

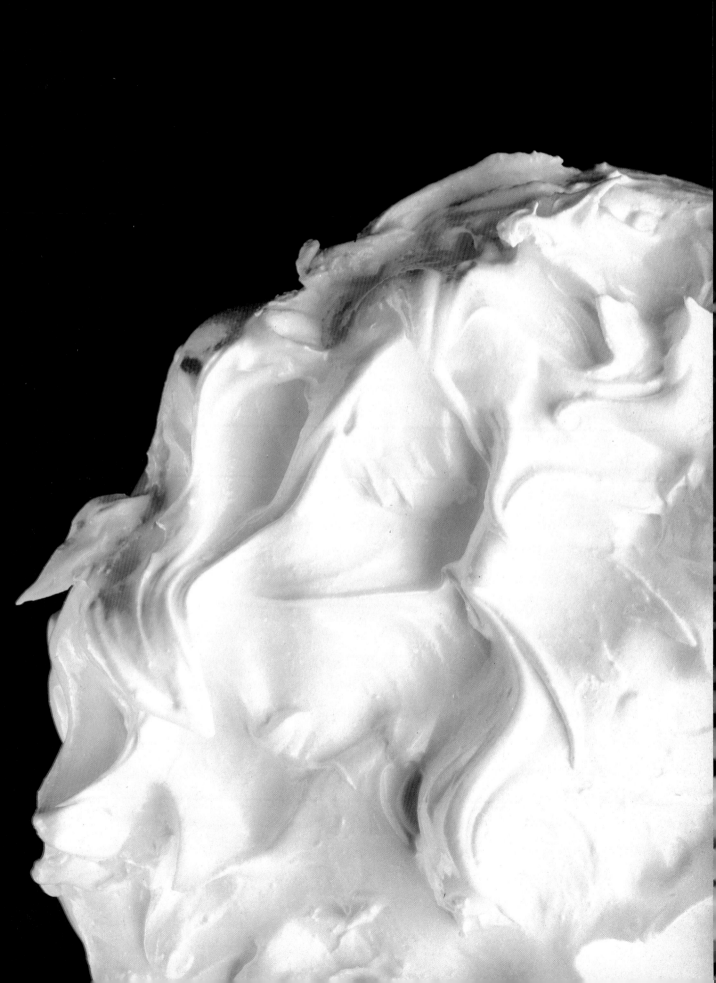

Mocha Frosting

Ingredients
30 g (1 oz) unsweetened chocolate
5 mL (1 teaspoon) lard
75 mL (1/3 cup) butter
1 egg
5 mL (1 teaspoon) vanilla
5 mL (1 teaspoon) instant coffee
5 mL (1 teaspoon) warm water
750 mL (3 cups) icing sugar

Method
— Melt the chocolate and the lard
  together at 30% for about 30 seconds.
  Set aside.
— Cream the butter and add the egg.
— Add the vanilla, coffee and warm
  water. Mix well.
— Gradually stir in the icing sugar and
  then the melted chocolate.
— Beat until smooth.

Japanese Frosting

Ingredients
125 mL (1/2 cup) lard
500 mL (2 cups) icing sugar
2 egg whites

Method
— Soften the lard by heating at 100% for
  1 minute.
— Add 125 mL (1/2 cup) icing sugar and
  beat well.
— Beat the egg whites until stiff and fold
  into the mixture.
— Gradually add the remaining icing
  sugar and mix well.
— Beat until creamy.
— Add a little more icing sugar if
  necessary.

Chocolate Frosting

Ingredients
90 g (3 oz) unsweetened chocolate
45 mL (3 tablespoons) butter
50 mL (1/4 cup) 35% cream
5 mL (1 teaspoon) vanilla
pinch salt
375 mL (1-1/2 cups) icing sugar

Method
— Melt the chocolate and the butter
  together at 70% for 1 to 2 minutes.
— Add the 35% cream, vanilla and salt.
— Gradually add the icing sugar and beat
  until smooth.

Cream Cheese Frosting

Ingredients
30 mL (2 tablespoons) butter
15 mL (1 tablespoon) 18 % cream
125 g (4 oz) cream cheese
400 to 500 mL (1-2/3 to 2 cups) icing
sugar

Method
— Blend the butter, cream and cream
  cheese and cook at 70% for 1 minute.
— Gradually add the icing sugar,
  thoroughly beating to a smooth
  texture.

Toppings

Nothing tempts lovers of good food quite as much as cakes and pastries. And it would seem that cooks take mischievous delight in making their creations look as appetizing as possible. But what is better—a feast for the eyes or a feast for the palate? Regrettably, we cannot avoid destroying the one in order to enjoy the other.

Fortunately, cooks are not dismayed by the demolition of their creations and they continue to produce for our enjoyment. However, even the most delicious cakes and pies depend on decorations and garnishes for their visual appeal.

Toppings, such as creams or meringues, are not meant as disguises but are eye-catching complements, having their own special flavors and textures. They come in all kinds of flavors.

Here are three simple recipes with which to begin. The results are sure to encourage you to try more.

Vanilla Topping

Level of Difficulty	🍴
Preparation Time	10 min
Cost per Serving	$
Yield	375 mL (1-1/2 cups) (enough for one cake)
Cooking Time	4 to 5 min for vanilla topping 5 to 6 min for chocolate topping
Standing Time	30 min
Power Level	100%
Write Your Cooking Time Here	

This chart applies to the recipe for chocolate topping as well.

Ingredients
50 mL (1/4 cup) sugar
30 mL (2 tablespoons) cornstarch
pinch salt
300 mL (1-1/4 cups) milk
15 mL (1 tablespoon) butter
5 mL (1 teaspoon) vanilla
2 egg yolks

Method
— Combine the sugar, cornstarch and salt. Stir in the milk.
— Cook at 100% for 4 to 5 minutes, stirring at 1 minute intervals, until the mixture thickens.
— Add the butter and stir until it melts. Then add the vanilla.
— Beat the egg yolks and add gradually, stirring continuously.
— Allow to cool for 30 minutes before using to decorate a cake.

Chocolate Topping

Ingredients
125 ml (1/2 cup) sugar
30 mL (2 tablespoons) cornstarch
pinch salt
300 mL (1-1/4 cups) milk
30 g (1 oz) unsweetened chocolate
15 mL (1 tablespoon) butter
2 egg yolks, beaten

Method
— Combine the sugar, cornstarch and salt. Add the milk to this mixture and stir.
— Cook at 100% for 4 to 5 minutes, stirring at 1 minute intervals, until the mixture thickens.
— Add the chocolate and stir well. Cook at 100% for 1 minute.
— Add the butter and stir until it melts.
— Gradually add the beaten egg yolks, stirring continuously.
— Allow to cool for 30 minutes before using to decorate a cake.

Lemon Topping

Level of Difficulty	▯▯▯
Preparation Time	5 min
Cost per Serving	$
Yield	300 mL (1-1/4 cups) (enough for one cake)
Cooking Time	2 to 3 min
Standing Time	none
Power Level	100%
Write Your Cooking Time Here	

Ingredients
75 mL (1/3 cup) sugar
22 mL (4-1/2 teaspoons) cornstarch
pinch salt
175 mL (3/4 cup) water
15 mL (1 tablespoon) butter
10 mL (2 teaspoons) lemon zest
45 mL (3 tablespoons) lemon juice

Method
— Combine the sugar, salt and cornstarch.
— Add the water gradually and cook at 100% for 2 to 3 minutes, or until the mixture thickens.
— Add the butter.
— Stir in the lemon zest and juice.

MICROTIPS

Substitutes

It is not uncommon to find yourself short of a vital ingredient for a recipe at the last minute. What can you do? Give up? Choose a different recipe? Fortunately, in many instances you can substitute one ingredient for another. Here are some substitutes that work well.

Butter or margarine	250 mL (1 cup)	250 mL (1 cup) shortening plus 2 mL (1/2 teaspoon) salt
Brown sugar	250 mL (1 cup)	175 mL (3/4 cup) white granulated sugar plus 50 mL (1/4 cup) molasses
Pastry flour	250 mL (1 cup) sifted	220 mL (7/8 cup) sifted all-purpose flour plus 7 mL (1-1/2 teaspoons) baking powder and 2 mL (1/2 teaspoon) salt
Honey	250 mL (1 cup)	250 mL (1 cup) sugar plus 50 mL (1/4 cup) liquid
Baking powder	5 mL (1 teaspoon)	1 mL (1/4 teaspoon) baking soda plus 3 mL (5/8 teaspoon) cream of tartar
Icing sugar	425 mL (1-3/4 cups)	250 mL (1 cup) granulated sugar
Grated lemon zest	5 mL (1 teaspoon)	2 mL (1/2 teaspoon) lemon extract

Puddings and Creams

Puddings and creams belong to Anglo-Saxon culinary traditions. As is typical of desserts, there is a great variety from which to choose and a range of corresponding preparation methods.

Both of these culinary delights owe their existence to one basic ingredient—eggs.

Puddings and creams can vary greatly in texture, depending on how they are made and how they are cooked. For example, some of these desserts use whole eggs, others use just the yolks and still others, the whites.

The versatility of eggs is quite astonishing, and cooks are constantly devising new and delicious recipes in which to use them.

Chocolate puddings, bread puddings, fruit puddings, puddings served with special sauces, caramelized puddings, glazed puddings . . . the list is endless. Creams are characteristically rich and smooth but can range in texture from set creams, which are desserts in their own right, to pouring creams, which are served with puddings.

These desserts, feasts for every occasion, can be served as everyday family desserts or at more formal celebrations. Some of the flambéed puddings are truly in the *cordon bleu* category and compare favorably with the finest French cuisine.

On the following pages you will find recipes that are easy to make. You will be able to make them confidently, time after time, to the delight of your family.

Rum Pudding Flambé

Level of Difficulty	🍴
Preparation Time	30 min
Cost per Serving	$ $ $
Yield	1 pudding, approximately 24 small servings
Cooking Time	12 to 14 min
Standing Time	10 to 15 min
Power Level	50%, 100%
Write Your Cooking Time Here	

Ingredients

Pudding:
125 mL (1/2 cup) molasses
175 mL (3/4 cup) brown sugar
10 mL (2 teaspoons) baking soda
250 mL (1 cup) candied fruit
125 mL (1/2 cup) raisins, soaked in water
75 mL (1/3 cup) rum
0.5 mL (1/8 teaspoon) nutmeg
pinch cinnamon
1 mL (1/4 teaspoon) salt
zest of 1/2 a lemon and 1/2 an orange
2 eggs
2 egg yolks
250 mL (1 cup) chopped suet
375 mL (1-1/2 cups) flour
250 mL (1 cup) breadcrumbs
175 mL (3/4 cup) milk

Glaze:
125 mL (1/2 cup) fruit jelly
icing sugar, to taste
125 mL (1/2 cup) rum

Method
— Combine the molasses, brown sugar and the baking soda. Add the candied fruit, raisins, rum, nutmeg, cinnamon, salt and the lemon and orange zest.
— Stir in the eggs, the egg yolks and the chopped suet.
— In another bowl mix the flour and breadcrumbs with the milk. Add to the sugar and fruit mixture, one-third at a time, stirring constantly.
— Put the batter into a tube pan.
— Place on a rack in the oven and cook at 50% for 6 minutes. Give the pan a half-turn and cook for a further 6 minutes, or until the pudding is done.
— Allow to stand for 10 to 15 minutes.
— Turn out by placing a

⟹

plate over the pan and then quickly turning upside down. The pudding should come away from the pan quite easily.
— Prepare the glaze by heating the fruit jelly at 100% for 45 seconds.
— Brush the melted jelly over the pudding and sprinkle with icing sugar.
— Heat the rum at 100% for 40 seconds. Pour over the pudding and ignite.

MICROTIPS

To Make Pudding From a Mix

Cooking pudding mixes in a microwave oven produces better results than when they are prepared in a conventional oven. The pudding is creamier and larger since less liquid evaporates in a microwave.

Cook puddings in microwave-safe measuring cups or ramekins for the best results.

Lazy Pudding

Ingredients

Pudding:
10 mL (2 teaspoons) butter
125 mL (1/2 cup) sugar
1 egg
250 mL (1 cup) flour
5 mL (1 teaspoon) baking powder
2 mL (1/2 teaspoon) salt
75 mL (1/3 cup) milk

Sauce:
500 mL (2 cups) brown sugar
250 mL (1 cup) water
10 mL (2 teaspoons) butter
125 mL (1/2 cup) flaked coconut

Method

— Combine all the ingredients for the sauce and bring to the boil by cooking at 100% for 4 to 6 minutes.
— Mix the butter and sugar and blend in the egg. Add the flour, baking powder and salt, alternately with the milk, stirring constantly.
— Pour the batter into a 20 cm (8 inch) square pan. Shield the corners of the pan with aluminum foil. Pour the sauce over the batter and place the pan on a rack in the oven.

Cook at 70% for 9 to 11 minutes, turning halfway through the cooking time. Let stand for 5 minutes. Serve with whipped cream.

Level of Difficulty	🍴
Preparation Time	10 min
Cost per Serving	$
Yield	1 pudding, approximately 8 servings
Cooking Time	15 to 17 min
Standing Time	5 min
Power Level	100%, 70%
Write Your Cooking Time Here	

Snowball Pudding

Ingredients

Pudding:
125 mL (1/2 cup) butter
250 mL (1 cup) sugar
550 mL (2-1/4 cups) flour

15 mL (1 tablespoon) baking powder
125 mL (1/2 cup) milk
4 egg whites

Caramel Sauce:
250 mL (1 cup) brown sugar
15 mL (1 tablespoon) flour
300 mL (1-1/4 cups) water
7 mL (1/2 tablespoon) butter
5 mL (1 teaspoon) vanilla

Level of Difficulty	🍴
Preparation Time	10 min
Cost per Serving	$
Yield	1 pudding, approximately 6 servings
Cooking Time	4 min
Standing Time	10 min
Power Level	70%
Write Your Cooking Time Here	✏️

Method
— Cream the butter, add the sugar and beat until smooth.
— Sift the flour and baking powder and add to the butter and sugar mixture, alternating with the milk.
— Beat the egg whites until stiff and fold them into the mixture.
— Brush individual tart or muffin pans with butter and pour the batter into them.
— Cover the pans with plastic wrap, place on a rack in the oven and cook at 70% for 4 minutes, turning halfway through the cooking time. Allow to stand for 10 minutes.
— Combine all the sauce ingredients and boil at 100% until the sauce turns golden.

Creams

Vanilla Cream

Ingredients
50 mL (1/4 cup) sugar
30 mL (2 tablespoons)
cornstarch
15 mL (1 tablespoon) flour
500 mL (2 cups) milk
4 egg yolks
30 mL (2 tablespoons) butter
2 mL (1/2 teaspoon) vanilla

Method
— Combine the sugar,
  cornstarch and flour.
— Add the milk to this
  mixture, stirring.
— Cook at 100% for 6
  minutes, or until the
  mixture thickens, stirring
  every 2 minutes.
— Beat the egg yolks and,
  stirring well, add 125 mL
  (1/2 cup) of the hot
  mixture to them.
— Add the remainder of the
  hot mixture and stir **again**.
— Cook at 100% for 1 to 2
  minutes, until the mixture
  is hot.
— Add the butter and vanilla
  and mix well.
— Place plastic wrap directly
  over the surface of the
  cream to prevent a skin
  from forming.
— Allow to cool before
  serving.

Chocolate Cream

Follow the recipe for vanilla cream but omit the sugar and butter. Instead, add 125 g (4 oz) semi-sweet chocolate chips (or grated chocolate) to the milk before you mix in the cornstarch and flour. Then proceed with the cooking. Garnish with whipped cream and shaved chocolate.

Strawberry Cream

Make vanilla cream and allow to cool. Purée 250 mL (1 cup) strawberries in a mixer and then stir 125 mL (1/2 cup) whipped cream into the purée. Stir into the vanilla cream. Garnish with sliced strawberries.

Caramel Cream

Follow the recipe for vanilla cream but use brown sugar instead of white and maple extract instead of vanilla extract. Add 45 mL (3 tablespoons) chopped walnuts before you proceed with the cooking.

Tips on How to Cut Calories

— Reduce the amount of sugar used by 25 mL (1/8 cup).
— Use 2% milk.
— Omit the butter.

Pies

The different kinds of pies that can be made are so numerous that their preparation calls for a full repertoire of culinary skills. The basis of any pie is pastry and pastry making is an art in its own right. Our mothers set great score by this skill. After satisfying their families with a chicken dinner and all the trimmings they would receive a chorus of compliments on the traditional apple pie dessert: ''Great pastry!'' It is not easy to master the special techniques required to make good pastry—most of us have done so only through constant practice.

But a pie is more than pastry. It is the filling that really counts, and Canadian culinary traditions favor sweet fillings. Fruit fillings are the most popular but fruit is not always in season.

Cooks have therefore devised such alternative fillings as cream fillings, chocolate fillings and cheese fillings, all of which are absolutely delicious and can be enjoyed all year long.

Pies, as other desserts, bring us a taste of the good life— novelty, extravagance and self-indulgence. They surely reign supreme in the realm of desserts in that they are more frequently served than any other type of dessert, on both formal and informal occasions.

In this volume on desserts you will find recipes for the most popular kinds of pies, ones that demonstrate a range of basic methods. The second dessert volume will include more complicated recipes. We hope that you will enjoy both making them and serving them.

Conventional Pie Crust

Ingredients
75 mL (1/3 cup) shortening
30 mL (2 tablespoons) butter
2 mL (1/2 teaspoon) salt
45 mL (3 tablespoons) *ice cold* water

250 mL (1 cup) all-purpose flour **OR** 175 mL (3/4 cup) whole wheat flour and 50 mL (1/4 cup) all-purpose flour

Although it should be very easy to make a successful pie crust, many of us have several failures before perfecting our technique. The method described here will help you attain success on your first try. Using a pastry blender, cut the shortening and butter into the flour and salt until the mixture resembles coarse crumbs. Add the water gradually, blending it in with a fork and shape the dough into a ball. To minimize shrinkage, allow the pastry to stand for 10 minutes to rest. Use a rolling pin to roll the pastry out and lay it over a pie plate.

Press the pastry against the sides of the pie plate to make room for the filling.

Use scissors to trim off excess pastry, leaving 2.5 (1 inch) extending over the edge of the pie plate.

Use your fingers to flute the edges, pressing every 1.25 cm (1/2 inch). This will give your pie crust a professional finish.

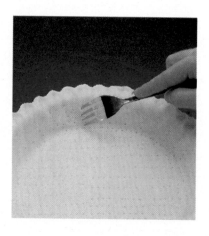

Prick the bottom and sides of the pastry with a fork. This step prevents the formation of air pockets between the pastry and the pie plate, which would cause the pastry to bubble and possibly crack during cooking.

To ensure that the pastry does not bubble, cover the base with dried peas. Place the pie plate on a rack or upturned saucer in the oven and cook at 70% for 6 minutes. Turn halfway through the cooking time. Test for doneness by checking the underside of the plate. The crust is cooked when the pastry is opaque.

Graham Crust

Ingredients
125 mL (1/2 cup) butter
325 mL (1-1/3 cups) Graham cracker crumbs
30 mL (2 tablespoons) brown sugar

Combine the butter, Graham crumbs and brown sugar. Mix the butter in very thoroughly.

Press the mixture onto the bottom and sides of a pie plate. Place on a rack in the oven and cook at 70% for 3 minutes. Turn halfway through the cooking time.

You can easily vary this type of pie crust by substituting a mixture of Corn Flakes, chocolate biscuits and a little ground ginger for the Graham crumbs.

There are a hundred and one ways to vary the color, taste and texture of pie crusts for microwave cooking. One obvious way is to substitute whole wheat flour for all-purpose flour, which makes quite a difference in the finished pastry. However, other ingredients can be added to the dough as well. Unless otherwise specified, add the following optional ingredients before rubbing the fat into the dry ingredients.

Coconut Crust: Add 125 mL (1/2 cup) flaked coconut. This pie crust goes well with cherry, rhubarb or cream fillings.

Spiced Crust: Add 15 mL (1 tablespoon) sugar, 5 mL (1 teaspoon) cinnamon and 1 mL (1/4 teaspoon) ground nutmeg. This crust is simply wonderful with cream or pastry cream fillings and also with pumpkin or apple.

Cheese Crust: Replace the butter with 125 mL (1/2 cup) grated cheddar cheese. Use with apple, pear or Chantilly cream fillings. It can also be used for quiches.

Coffee Crust: Add 5 or 10 mL (1 or 2 teaspoons) instant coffee dissolved in a little water as well as 30 mL (2 tablespoons) finely chopped pecans. This variation complements the taste of cream fillings.

Nut Crust: Add 50 mL (1/4 cup) chopped nuts and 1 mL (1/4 teaspoon) ground nutmeg. Excellent with cream fillings.

Chocolate Crust: Add 15 mL (1 tablespoon) sugar and 30 mL (2 tablespoons) cocoa. Use with chocolate fillings.

Apple Pie

Level of Difficulty	
Preparation Time	15 min
Cost per Serving	$ $
Yield	1 pie, approximately 8 servings
Cooking Time	4 min
Standing Time	None
Power Level	90%
Write Your Cooking Time Here	

Ingredients
1 pie crust, cooked
15 mL (1 tablespoon) cornstarch
30 mL (2 tablespoons) flour
125 mL (1/2 cup) sugar
2 mL (1/2 teaspoon) cinnamon
15 mL (1 tablespoon) butter
1.25 L (5 cups) apples, peeled and cut into pieces
125 mL (1/2 cup) Harvest Crunch type cereal

Method
— Combine the cornstarch, flour, sugar and cinnamon. Put one-third of the mixture into the cooked pie crust.
— Add the apples and the remaining mixture.
— Dot small pieces of butter on top of the pie and sprinkle the cereal over top.
— Place on a rack in the oven and cook at 90% for 2 minutes. Turn the plate and cook at 90% for a further 2 minutes.

Assemble the ingredients required for this traditional dessert, which is easy to make and always popular.

Combine all the dry ingredients except the cereal, and put one-third of the mixture into the cooked pie crust. Add the apple pieces.

Add the remaining mixture of cornstarch, flour, sugar and cinnamon. Dot small pieces of butter on top of the pie and add the cereal.

Place a piece of waxed paper under the pie plate to protect the oven from any spills. Cook at 90% for 4 minutes, turning halfway through the cooking time.

Sugar Pie

Level of Difficulty	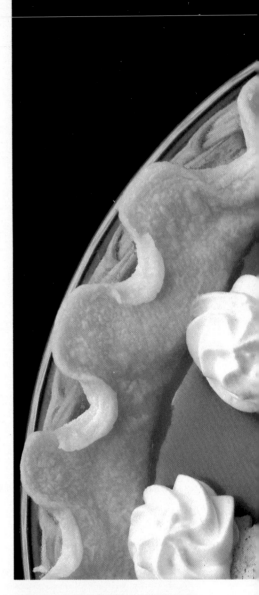
Preparation Time	10 min
Cost per Serving	$ $
Yield	1 pie, approximately 8 servings
Cooking Time	10 to 12 min
Standing Time	10 min
Power Level	100%, 90%
Write Your Cooking Time Here	

Ingredients
1 pie crust, cooked
500 mL (2 cups) brown sugar
60 mL (4 tablespoons) flour
15 mL (1 tablespoon) butter
15 mL (1 tablespoon) corn syrup
250 mL (1 cup) milk
pie pastry, uncooked
pinch cinnamon
pinch sugar

Method
— Combine the brown sugar with the flour and stir in the butter, corn syrup and milk.
— Cook at 100% for 8 to 10 minutes, or until the mixture thickens. Stir once during the cooking time.

Let stand 10 minutes after cooking.
— Pour the mixture into the cooked pie crust. Set aside.
— Using a pastry wheel, cut strips of pastry and weave them into a lattice on waxed paper.
— Sprinkle with cinnamon and sugar, place on a rack in the oven, and cook at 90% for 2 minutes.
— Place the cooked lattice on top of the pie.

The ingredients you require are a cooked pie crust, milk, corn syrup, butter, flour and brown sugar.

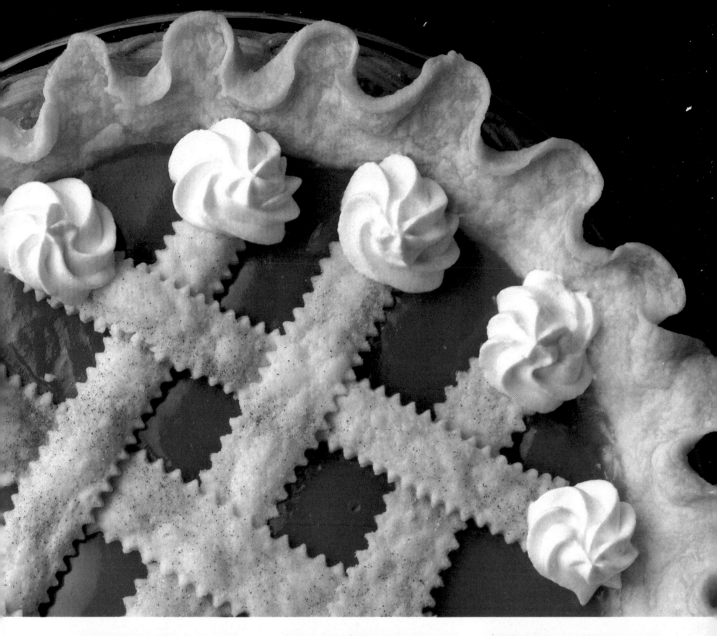

Cook the mixture of brown sugar, flour, butter, corn syrup and milk. Pour into the pie crust.

Use a pastry wheel to cut strips of uncooked pastry.

Weave the pastry strips into a lattice, sprinkle with cinnamon and sugar and cook at 90% for 2 minutes.

Strawberry Pie

Ingredients
1 pie crust, cooked
125 mL (1/2 cup) sugar
22 mL (1-1/2 tablespoons)
cornstarch
1 284 mL (10 oz) package
frozen strawberries
15 mL (1 tablespoon) lemon
juice
fresh strawberries for garnish

Method
— Combine all the
  ingredients for the filling
  except the fresh
  strawberries.
— Cook at 100% for 5 to 7
  minutes, or until the
  mixture thickens, stirring
  every 2 minutes.
— Pour the mixture into the
  cooked pie crust.
— Let stand in the
  refrigerator for 2 hours.
— Decorate with the fresh
  strawberries before
  serving.

Level of Difficulty	🍴
Preparation Time	10 min
Cost per Serving	$ $
Yield	1 pie, approximately 8 servings
Cooking Time	5 to 7 min
Standing Time	2 hr in the refrigerator
Power Level	100%
Write Your Cooking Time Here	

Peach Pie

Ingredients
1 pie crust, cooked
1.25 L (5 cups) peaches,
sliced
150 mL (2/3 cup) sugar
30 mL (2 tablespoons)
cornstarch

50 mL (1/4 cup) water
30 mL (2 tablespoons) lemon
juice

Method
— Purée 250 mL (1 cup)
  peaches in a blender.
— Combine the sugar,
  cornstarch, water and
  lemon juice. Blend in the
  puréed peaches.
— Cook at 100% for 2
  minutes. Stir thoroughly
  and continue to cook at
  100% for 4 to 6 minutes,
  or until the mixture
  thickens, stirring at
  1 minute intervals.
— Pour this mixture into the
  cooked pie crust and lay
  the remaining peach slices
  on top.
— Let stand in the
  refrigerator for 2 hours
  before serving.

Level of Difficulty	🍴
Preparation Time	15 min
Cost per Serving	$ $
Yield	1 pie, approximately 8 servings
Cooking Time	6 to 8 min
Standing Time	2 hr in the refrigerator
Power Level	100%
Write Your Cooking Time Here	

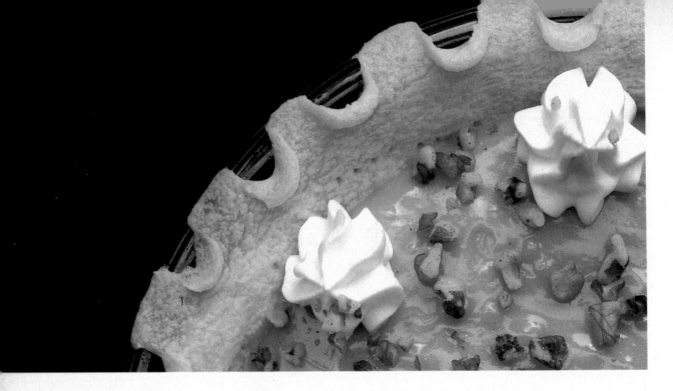

Maple Cream Pie

Ingredients
1 pie crust, cooked
250 mL (1 cup) maple syrup
250 mL (1 cup) milk
30 mL (2 tablespoons) butter
45 mL (3 tablespoons) cornstarch
50 mL (1/4 cup) cold water
2 egg yolks, beaten
5 mL (1 teaspoon) vanilla

Method
— Combine the maple syrup, milk and butter, mix well and cook at 100% for 3 minutes.
— Mix the cornstarch with the cold water and stir in the beaten egg yolks and vanilla. Add to the hot syrup mixture, beating constantly.
— Cook at 100% for 6 minutes, stirring very thoroughly every 2 minutes.
— Allow to stand for 15 minutes and pour into the cooked pie crust.
— Decorate with whipped cream and walnut pieces before serving.

Level of Difficulty	🍴
Preparation Time	10 min
Cost per Serving	$ $
Yield	1 pie, approximately 8 servings
Cooking Time	9 min
Standing Time	15 min
Power Level	100%
Write Your Cooking Time Here	

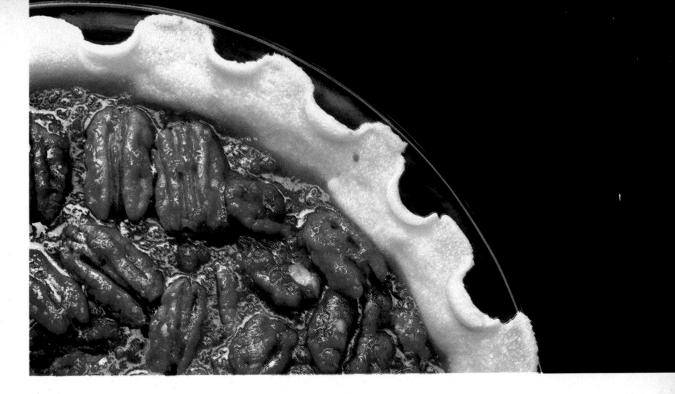

Pecan Pie

Ingredients
1 pie crust, cooked
3 eggs
125 mL (1/2 cup) brown sugar
250 mL (1 cup) corn syrup
30 mL (2 tablespoons) butter
15 mL (1 tablespoon) flour
5 mL (1 teaspoon) vanilla
1 mL (1/4 teaspoon) salt
375 mL (1-1/2 cups) pecans

Method
— Beat one egg yolk until it is foamy and brush it over the cooked pie crust.
— Cook at 100% for 30 to 40 seconds. Set aside.
— Beat the remaining egg white and 2 whole eggs. Add all the other ingredients except the pecans.
— Stir until smooth and then add half the pecans.
— Cook at 100% for 2 minutes. Stir and continue to cook at 100% for another 4 minutes.
— Reduce the power level to 50% and cook for 6 more minutes, stirring halfway through the cooking time.
— Add the remaining pecans and cook at 50% for 3 minutes, or until the mixture thickens.
— Allow to stand for 15 minutes and pour into the cooked pie crust.

Level of Difficulty	🍴
Preparation Time	10 min
Cost per Serving	$ $
Yield	1 pie, approximately 8 servings
Cooking Time	15 min
Standing Time	15 min
Power Level	100%, 50%
Write Your Cooking Time Here	

Lemon Meringue Pie

Level of Difficulty	🍴🍴
Preparation Time	20 min
Cost per Serving	$ $
Yield	1 pie, approximately 8 servings
Cooking Time	15 to 17 min
Standing Time	10 min
Power Level	100%, 70%
Write Your Cooking Time Here	

Ingredients
1 pie crust, cooked
375 mL (1-1/2 cups) sugar
75 mL (1/3 cup) cornstarch
0.5 mL (1/8 teaspoon) salt
500 mL (2 cups) cold water
grated zest of 1 lemon
50 mL (1/4 cup) margarine
or butter
4 egg yolks
125 mL (1/2 cup) lemon juice
4 egg whites
2 mL (1/2 teaspoon)
cornstarch

Method
— In a large bowl, mix 250 mL (1 cup) sugar, 75 mL (1/3 cup) cornstarch and the salt. Stir well to remove any lumps and then add the water and lemon zest.
— Mix well and cook at 100% for 7 minutes, or until the mixture boils and turns clear. Stir frequently during the cooking time.
— Add the butter or margarine and stir until melted.
— In a small bowl, beat the egg yolks and stir in the lemon juice. Add a small amount to the cooked ingredients. Stir well and then add the remaining egg yolk to the cooked mixture.
— Cook at 100% for 4 to 5 minutes, or until the mixture thickens. Pour the mixture into the pie crust.
— Put the egg whites and the 2 mL (1/2 teaspoon) cornstarch into a large bowl and beat with an electric beater at high speed.

- Continue beating as you gradually add the 125 mL (1/2 cup) remaining sugar.
- Beat until stiff.
- Carefully spread the meringue over the lemon filling.
- Place on a rack in the oven and cook at 70% for 3 to 5 minutes, giving the plate a half-turn halfway through the cooking time.
- Allow to stand for 10 minutes before serving.

MICROTIPS

To Prevent a Pie Crust from Going Soggy

To prevent a pie crust from going soggy when you add the filling, simply brush over the inner surface with a beaten egg yolk and heat for a few seconds in the microwave oven.

To Melt Chocolate

Many cakes, pastries and ice creams will be all the more delicious if they are topped with melted chocolate. You can melt chocolate in the microwave without having to use a double boiler. Simply arrange pieces of chocolate on a microwave-safe plate and heat them at 50% for 2 minutes.

All Things Nice

Sugar and spice make all things nice. Not only nice, but irresistible. Surely we have all succumbed at one time or another to the temptation of a gorgeous dessert. We have only to see one for our mouths to begin to water in anticipation.

The repertoire of sweet desserts is not limited to such classics as cakes and pies. Fruit crisps, fondues and squares all vie for our attention. This final section contains a mouth-watering selection to round off our gastronomic tour.

Here you will find such perennial favorites as date squares, apple crisp, chocolate mousse and chocolate fondue. We also offer a recipe for pastry cream, which can be used in an infinite number of desserts.

We have a background of cultural diversity to thank for the fact that we can choose from such a stunning array of desserts. We should try to preserve this diversity in our cooking; it is a statement about our identity and a source of considerable pleasure. Our children are bound to thank us for passing this legacy on to them.

Fruit Flan
with Pastry Cream

Level of Difficulty	🍴🥄
Preparation Time	35 min
Cost per Serving	$ $
Yield	approximately 20 servings
Cooking Time	13 min
Standing Time	None
Power Level	50%, 100%
Write Your Cooking Time Here	✏️🍎

Ingredients
2 eggs, beaten
250 mL (1 cup) sugar
15 mL (1 tablespoon) butter
250 mL (1 cup) flour
pinch salt
5 mL (1 teaspoon) baking powder
125 mL (1/2 cup) hot milk
fresh and canned fruit
cornstarch

Method
— Combine the beaten eggs, sugar and butter and beat until smooth.
— Sift the flour, salt and baking powder and stir into the egg mixture, alternately with the milk. Begin and end with the dry ingredients.
— Line a pizza plate with the flan base, spreading it evenly.
— Cook at 50% for 7 to 8 minutes. Top with pastry cream (recipe, p. 100).
— Drain the juice from the fruit and set aside.
— Arrange the fruit on the pastry cream.
—Stir the cornstarch into the fruit juice and cook at 100% until it thickens, approximately 2 to 3 minutes.
—Pour the glaze over the fruit and serve.

Assemble all the ingredients required for this delicious fruit dessert, which you can make in both winter and summer.

Basic Method for Pastry Cream
Mix the salt, milk and vanilla. Cook at 100 % until hot, stirring every two minutes.

Beat the eggs thoroughly. Stirring continuously, gradually add the cornstarch mixture.

Cook the mixture and cover it with plastic wrap to prevent a skin from forming while you cook the fruit juice.

Pastry Cream

Ingredients
500 mL (2 cups) milk
4 drops vanilla extract
1 mL (1/4 teaspoon) salt
175 mL (3/4 cup) sugar
75 mL (1/3 cup) cornstarch
2 eggs

Method
— Combine the milk, vanilla and salt and cook at 100% until the liquid is hot, stirring every 2 minutes.
— Mix in the cornstarch and the sugar and set aside.
— Beat the eggs thoroughly and then gradually stir in the milk mixture. Stir continuously to prevent lumps from forming.
— Cook at 100% for 3 to 4 minutes, or until the mixture thickens, stirring at 1 minute intervals.
— Place a piece of plastic wrap directly on the surface of the cream to prevent a skin from forming.

Chocolate Mousse

Ingredients
300 mL (1-1/4 cups) 35%
cream
1 175 g (6 oz) package
unsweetened chocolate chips
125 mL (1/2 cup) sugar
3 egg yolks
3 egg whites
7 mL (1-1/2 teaspoons)
vanilla
1 mL (1/4 teaspoon) salt
1 mL (1/4 teaspoon) cream
of tartar
fresh raspberries or curls of
orange zest and chocolate to
garnish

Method
— Select a 1 L (4 cup) glass
measure and combine the
cream, chocolate chips
and half of the sugar.
Cook at 100% for 2-1/2
to 4 minutes, or until the
chocolate has melted. Stir
once or twice during the
cooking.
— Beat the egg yolks with 5
mL (1 teaspoon) vanilla
and the salt, until thick
and pale.
— Add the melted chocolate
mixture. Mix well and set

in the refrigerator.
— Beat the egg whites with
the remaining vanilla and
the cream of tartar, until
foamy.
— Gradually add the
remaining sugar and beat
until the mixture stands
up in stiff peaks.
— Fold into the chocolate
mixture until thoroughly
blended.
— Pour into cream molds or
individual dessert cups.
Refrigerate.

Almond Cream

Ingredients
175 mL (3/4 cup) cold water
1 envelope unflavored gelatin
125 mL (1/2 cup) sugar
175 mL (3/4 cup) boiling
water
300 mL (1-1/4 cups)
evaporated milk
2 mL (1/2 teaspoon) vanilla
2 mL (1/2 teaspoon) almond
extract
fresh fruit, optional

Method
— Pour the cold water into a
  small bowl and sprinkle
  with the gelatin. Let stand
  for 1 minute. Add the
  sugar and stir to dissolve.
— Pour the boiling water*
  into a medium bowl and
  add the gelatin mixture,
  stirring constantly.
— Combine the evaporated
  milk, vanilla and almond

extract. Add to the gelatin
mixture, stirring
constantly.
— Pour the almond cream
  into dessert cups and leave
  for 3 hours in the
  refrigerator. If you wish,
  decorate with fresh fruit
  before serving.

* Boil the water by heating it at 100% for 3 to
3-1/2 minutes

Strawberry Mousse

Ingredients
175 mL (3/4 cup) sugar
500 mL (2 cups) water
50 mL (1/4 cup) honey
250 mL (1 cup) strawberries,
crushed
15 mL (1 tablespoon) lemon
juice

Method
— Blend the sugar, water
  and honey and heat at
  100% until it boils.
— Continue to cook until the
  mixture becomes syrupy,
  stirring every 2 minutes.
— Allow to stand for 10
  minutes, and then add the

strawberries and lemon
juice and mix.
— Place in the freezer for 1
  or 2 hours to become
  firm, stirring every 10
  minutes to prevent crystals
  from forming.

Chocolate Fondue

Ingredients
300 g (10 oz) milk chocolate
300 mL (1-1/4 cups) 35%
cream
50 mL (1/4 cup) honey
60 g (2 oz) ground hazelnuts

Method
— Grate the milk chocolate.
— Add all the other
  ingredients and mix well.
— Cook at 50%, until the
  ingredients have melted
  together, stirring every
  minute.

Apple Crisp

Ingredients
1.25 L (5 cups) apple, peeled and coarsely chopped
cinnamon to taste
nutmeg to taste

50 mL (1/4 cup) butter
250 mL (1 cup) Special K, partially crumbled
125 mL (1/2 cup) dark brown sugar

15 mL (1 tablespoon) flour

Level of Difficulty	
Preparation Time	10 min
Cost per Serving	$
Yield	8 servings
Cooking Time	4 min 30 s
Standing Time	3 min
Power Level	100%
Write Your Cooking Time Here	

Method
— Arrange the apple pieces in a serving dish and sprinkle with cinnamon and nutmeg to taste.
— Melt the butter at 100% for 30 seconds.
— Combine the Special K, brown sugar and flour and then add the melted butter. Sprinkle over the apples.
— Place the dish, uncovered, on a rack in the oven and cook at 100% for 4 minutes. Turn halfway through the cooking time. Allow to stand for 3 minutes before serving.

Date Squares

Level of Difficulty	ᵗⁱ
Preparation Time	20 min
Cost per Serving	$ $
Yield	approximately 18 squares
Cooking Time	14 min
Standing Time	at least 15 min
Power Level	100%, 70%
Write Your Cooking Time Here	

Ingredients

Crust:
250 mL (1 cup) butter or margarine
250 mL (1 cup) brown sugar
375 mL (1-1/2 cups) flour
5 mL (1 teaspoon) baking powder
1 mL (1/4 teaspoon) salt
375 mL (1-1/2 cups) rolled oats

Date Filling:
500 g (1-1/4 lb) dates, pitted
250 mL (1 cup) pineapple, crushed, in its juice

Method
— Begin by preparing the date filling. Chop the dates and add the pineapple and juice. Cook at 100% for 4 minutes. Purée in a blender and set aside.
— For the crust, cream the butter with the brown sugar. Add all the other ingredients and mix well.
— Put half this mixture into a baking dish and spread evenly. Cover with the date and pineapple filling, and then top with the remaining crust mixture.
— Place on a rack in the oven and cook at 70% for 10 minutes. Turn halfway through the cooking time. Let stand at least 15 minutes.

MICROTIPS

Cooking with Sugar

If your mixture contains a lot of sugar, take care not to cook it for longer than the recipe directs. Sugar can quickly get too hot, at which point it may burn.

To Maximize the Volume of Egg White

Egg white that has been kept in the refrigerator has considerably less potential for volume than egg white at room temperature. You can get around this problem by heating the egg white in the microwave at 100% for 5 seconds. Do not heat for any longer or it will explode.

To Unmold a Frozen Dessert

Unmolding a frozen dessert can be tricky. A simple method is to chill the serving plate, place it over the mold and quickly turn the whole thing upside down. Lift the mold off carefully.

Food Storage Times

There are several ways to store food. Some types of food keep well in the pantry whereas others must be refrigerated or frozen. Here is a chart to help you plan both your shopping and your cooking with a minimum of waste.

Food	Time	Comments
Baking soda	over 2 years	dry, covered
Bread	5 days	to keep bread crusty, do not wrap in plastic to store
Breadcrumbs	6 months	dry, covered
Flour, corn	12 months	dry, sealed
Flour, whole wheat	6 to 8 months	refrigerated, in a sealed container
Honey	12 months	crystallization is not a sign that the honey has gone bad
Nuts, unshelled	6 months	
Peanut butter	6 to 9 months	
Sugar, brown	6 months	refrigerated, in a sealed container
Sugar, white	over 2 years	dry, in a sealed container

In the Refrigerator	Time	Comments
Eggs, in their shells	1 or 2 weeks	store covered and with the broad end uppermost so the yolk stays in the center
Butter, margarine	2 weeks	may also be frozen for longer storage
Cream cheese	7 to 10 days	keep wrapped
Sour cream	1 week	

In the Freezer		
Butter	5 to 6 months	
Sour cream	not recommended	
Milk	1 month	
Cookies	about 1 year	
Cheesecake	4 months	
Ordinary cakes	4 to 6 months	
Yeast breads	up to 12 months	
Muffins	1 to 2 months	
Fruit pies	3 to 4 months	
Pie crusts	1-1/2 to 2 months	

Dessert Terminology

Caramelize: Caramel is sugar that has been dissolved in twice its volume of water and cooked until golden brown. You can caramelize sauces and creams by adding caramel to them. Another way to caramelize a dessert is to coat the interior of the pan with caramel, so that it will form a coating when the dessert is turned out. Or you can cover a dessert with sugar and then melt the sugar under the broiler until it caramelizes.

Cream: Slowly beating together butter or margarine and sugar will make the mixture fluffy and soft.

Crumbs: Stale bread, cakes and cookies can be crushed with a rolling pin to produce fine crumbs that are useful for decorating certain types of desserts.

Dip: Cakes, cookies and pastries may be dipped in melted chocolate or fondant mix to produce a decorative coating.

Flambé: When a dessert is served flambé, it is first covered with an alcoholic liquor and then served alight.

Glaze: You glaze a dessert when you give it a glossy finish. There are a variety of glazes, such as syrup, fondant and frosting. A glaze for pastry consists of eggs beaten with either milk or water and brushed on before baking. This type of glaze gives pastry a lovely golden appearance.

Knead: Kneading is the hand process used for combining a stiff dough.

Line: You line a dish when you cover it with a thin layer of pastry to form a pie crust.

Pie crust: A pie crust is a shell of pastry that lines the plate and holds the filling.

Purée: You purée ingredients in order to blend them until they are of a uniform, smooth consistency.

Thin: You thin a batter, sauce or cream by adding additional liquid or semi-liquid ingredients such as butter, eggs and cream.

Conversion Chart

**Conversion Chart for the
Main Measures Used in
Cooking**

Volume		Weight	
1 teaspoon	5 mL	2.2 lb	1 kg (1000 g)
1 tablespoon	15 mL	1.1 lb	500 g
		0.5 lb	225 g
1 quart (4 cups)	1 litre	0.25 lb	115 g
1 pint (2 cups)	500 mL		
1/2 cup	125 mL		
1/4 cup	50 mL	1 oz	30 g

**Metric Equivalents
for Cooking
Temperatures**

49°C	120°F	120°C	250°F
54°C	130°F	135°C	275°F
60°C	140°F	150°C	300°F
66°C	150°F	160°C	325°F
71°C	160°F	180°C	350°F
77°C	170°F	190°C	375°F
82°C	180°F	200°C	400°F
93°C	200°F	220°C	425°F
107°C	225°F	230°C	450°F

Readers will note that, in the recipes, we give 250 mL as the equivalent for 1 cup and 450 g as the equivalent for 1 lb and that fractions of these measurements are even less mathematically accurate. The reason for this is that mathematically accurate conversions are just not practical in cooking. Your kitchen scales are simply not accurate enough to weigh 454 g—the true equivalent of 1 lb—and it would be a waste of time to try. The conversions given in this series, therefore, necessarily represent approximate equivalents, but they will still give excellent results in the kitchen. No problems should be encountered if you adhere to either metric or imperial measurements throughout a recipe.

Index